One of Us

One of Us

Single People as Part of the Church

Steve Chilcraft

WORD PUBLISHING
Nelson Word Ltd
Milton Keynes, England

WORD AUSTRALIA
Kilsyth, Victoria, Australia

WORD COMMUNICATIONS LTD
Vancouver, B.C., Canada

STRUIK CHRISTIAN BOOKS (PTY) LTD
Maitland, South Africa

JOINT DISTRIBUTORS SINGAPORE –
ALBY COMMERCIAL ENTERPRISES PTE LTD
and
CAMPUS CRUSADE

CHRISTIAN MARKETING NEW ZEALAND LTD
Havelock North, New Zealand

JENSCO LTD
Hong Kong

SALVATION BOOK CENTRE
Malaysia

To all members of the Singularly Significant Committee, past and present, who have done so much to deepen my understanding of the subject of singleness.

To my own parents and family for their lifelong love and support.

To Eric and Betty and Clive and Ruth who took in a homeless bachelor many years ago.

Contents

Contents

About the Authors

John Littlewood is the vicar of Christ Church, Highbury, North London. He was raised in York. After school, he joined a small professional office of surveyors and auctioneers. He was converted in his late twenties. He has served in parishes in Northamptonshire and Peterborough and as Chaplain to Scargill House in North Yorkshire. He is a lifelong bachelor, and co-editor of the *Singularly Significant* bulletin.

As General Director of the Saltmine Trust, **Dave Pope** oversees the day-to-day running of the Trust as well as travelling all over Britain in a ministry of evangelism and Bible teaching. He graduated from the University of Aston with a B.Sc. in Behavioural Sciences. He joined the Movement for World Evangelisation in 1970. In 1980 he formed the Saltmine Trust. He is also a member of the Spring Harvest Executive Committee. Dave is well known as a gifted worship leader. He is a member of the Singularly Significant committee. He is single. His hobbies include reading, tennis and visiting Indian restaurants. He is a very keen amateur gardener.

Sheena Gillies, who is single, is Associate Director of Pastoring at All Souls, Langham Place in London. She is involved in the supporting and training of leaders of small groups within the church. She works with all ages, providing general counselling and pastoring support. Previously a teacher, Sheena also spent seven years as a Director of Training at London Bible College.

Roger Welch has been minister of Tottenham Corner Evangelical Free Church in Surrey for the last twelve years. He has a degree in History from the University of Kent. He taught in a grammar school prior to his call to the ministry. He is a chairman of the British Council of Wycliffe Bible Translators. He is married to Diane and has two children. He is a member of the Singularly Significant committee.

Dave Richards is senior pastor of the Basingstoke Community Church in Hampshire. A former teacher, he travels widely speaking on leadership, discipleship, missions and the Holy Spirit. He is married to Chris. He is a keen cricketer and Manchester United supporter.

Foreword

S ome years ago, while living in Milton Keynes, Ruth and I welcomed a temporary addition to the household. Steve, the author of this book, was an old friend who needed somewhere to stay for the night—he left three months later!

Steve was travelling extensively as a regional co-ordinator for a well known Christian organisation. He was purchasing his own home and expected to move before long. As often happens with Steve it all took longer than expected.

Ruth and I have always adopted the policy that a family goes beyond physical and nuclear boundaries. The fact that someone happens to be unmarried can scarcely deprive them of 'family' status. Consequently we have enjoyed the privilege of people living with us for much of our married lives.

Our children have tended towards the same attitude. During Steve's sojourn with us, as Christmas approached, Gavin (then our youngest child) was asked a simple question: 'Who is your family?' He thought for a moment. 'Mummy, Daddy . . . Vicky, Kristen . . . Tozer [the dog] . . . and Steve.' Such was the accurate assessment of family life from the lips of a three year old. His family included a bachelor friend of his parents who was enduring temporary residence!

I long for all to share Gavin's wisdom. For somehow large sections of the church have lost their way on the issue of incorporating single people. Too often the word 'family' has come to mean parents and young children. In the life of the church it should rather refer to a glorious hotch-potch of adolescents, married, formerly married, widowed, single by choice and the not-yet married, all seeking to share and operate together in the household of God.

It is to help in addressing this need that the book you are about to read was written. It comes, in part, from an originally felt need which was expressed, some years ago, to the Evangelical Alliance. In response, a consultation was called—this led to the formation of a coalition of those involved in singles ministry. This group, Singularly Significant, is itself an important statement of the Alliance. The publications and initiatives which it has sponsored are a crucial step forward in acknowledging that as evangelical Christians we have an important task ahead of us.

I believe that single people have been largely ignored, marginalised and uncatered for in much of our church life. This has not been conscious neglect. It was never intended to imply rejection. But often that has been the unfortunate result of our conduct.

Writing from years of personal experience as a long-standing bachelor, Steve has much to share. Yet, as one who is now married he does not speak from personal rancour but sincere conviction. His years on Singularly Significant have provided a wider perspective. He believes that repentance for our past failures is necessary, but also that the potential exists for a new dawn in our church relationships.

I share his hope. I trust that this volume with its humour, provocation, analysis and practical guidance, tinged with sadness, will prove to be a source of stimulus and encouragement to all its readers.

Clive Calver
London, 1993

Preface

This book is a team effort. I have been a member of an Evangelical Alliance committee, focusing on single people, since it started in 1986. The group, aptly entitled Singularly Significant, was formed to look at the issue of singleness in the British church. This book is a result of the development of my own appreciation of the subject. Singularly Significant is a coalition—it seeks to reflect the diverse views of single people. Within this book this diversity will be found—we do not agree in detail about every issue and that is not our aim. The purpose is to draw attention to a great perceived need which, together, we want to do something about.

It was with the enthusiastic support of the committee that I embarked on this project, but for better or worse the responsibility is my own. The first four chapters are my own work. In Chapters 5 to 9 I invited five friends to give their personal perspective on a range of issues. I am most grateful to all of them for their hard work. Everyone has expressed their own views and those should not be misread as necessarily representing the views of all Singularly Significant members.

I thank Clive Calver, the General Director of the Evangelical Alliance, for his Foreword. Clive is married with four children, yet it was he who responded to a challenge to look at the issue of singleness in the British church, and called together the group which subsequently became Singularly Significant. His continued support and deep awareness of issues which concern single Christians is much appreciated.

I also want to thank my friends who contributed to the first chapter. Their honesty and integrity is priceless. Many, if not most, found the exercise painful. It touched nerves, brought out old and present wounds, fears as well as hopes. Without them *One of Us* would be much the poorer.

I thank Administry for permission to use material from their excellent report 'Single-minded' in Chapter 3, and for the use of the cartoons which grace these pages.

Some readers may question why a married man is writing about singleness. I believe this is an issue for the whole church. This book is not a platform for single people to moan about all that is wrong in the church. It is an attempt to give an overview, a platform for the whole church to take action. Unless married people see the need for change nothing will happen. This is an issue for us all—single and married solidly together. We are the church; if one part is suffering we all suffer. It was as a long-term bachelor that I became interested in singleness in the church, because I believed it was an issue of both truth and justice. I believe it requires urgent attention. My own marriage has not changed this conviction at all.

I thank my wife Ruth for her own insights on singleness, her support throughout the writing of the book, her long hours at the word processor late into the night and for her love. She sometimes complains that she is the only person in the world married to a single man. In the final stages of preparing the manuscript, it is a case of many a true word being spoken in jest!

I thank those at Word Publishing, especially Noël Halsey, Linda Finley-Day, Beth Bissett, Alison Jenkins, Win Kennedy and Lee Morris, for their encouragement, patience and commitment.

Finally, thanks to all those who have set an example by their love and support of single Christians. We appreciate all you have given. Jesus has come to us through you.

Milton Keynes, April 1993

Introduction

No one likes to be excluded. We all need to belong. Yet in the church there can be people who, although members of the congregation, feel they do not belong. If this is the case something must be wrong, since the true church is entirely made up of those accepted by Christ.

All too frequently I hear the complaint from single Christians that they feel like second-class citizens in their church. Not that the church itself believes it treats them so—the accusation is normally vociferously denied. This is part of the problem: no one deliberately excludes people just because they are single—it is normally due to neglect or thoughtlessness rather than intent. Many singles feel hurt. It is time for corrective action. Single people need to know that their own church regards them as 'one of us', fully accepted just as they are.

There are four reasons why it is important for the church to consider singleness at this time. Firstly, the issue is not an abstract concept but is about people; individuals with their own potential, problems and personality. If any section of the Body of Christ asks for help we must be ready to respond. If a regular stream of people come echoing similar concerns we must suspect a strategic weakness.

Secondly, the world around us is changing fast. There is a major demographic shift occurring throughout the Western world. The number of single people is growing rapidly. We need to know what is happening in order to know how to respond.

Thirdly, local churches have always constructed their life around the nuclear family. Unseen by most, the number of single adults in the congregation has grown as the percentage of single people in society has grown. The church has not adapted to meet this change.

Fourthly, most Christians have little understanding of the Bible's teaching about singleness. There has been much teaching in recent years about marriage and family life but not about celibacy. There is a need to rediscover a scriptural perspective and to apply this to our generation.

The first four chapters of this book seek to address these issues. Thereafter five Christian leaders, both single and married, committed to improving the current situation, give their personal perspectives on some of the most important aspects of singleness within the church today. The last chapter includes a plan of action for the local church and a call for change.

Most books on singleness are written from a personal point of view and are directed at the single person individually. This work is different. It tackles different ground. The writers hope that it will be of real help to a great many single people who read it. But that is not our prime goal. We want all sorts of Christians to read it: church leaders, house group leaders, anyone who has single friends, of any age or category, and has a desire to help them in their Christian life. We believe there is a need for change. We hope *One of Us* will help many churches to rethink their approach to singleness. We hope it is a positive contribution to a growing concern for the 35 per cent of British Christians who are single.

If as a result of reading *One of Us* your church is helped to help its own single people, we shall have succeeded. That is our prayer.

1

Meet My Friends

*Being single is not God's second best. It is a gift from
God and He does not give second-rate gifts.*

Trevor Partridge

*Fulfilment and marriage are not to be treated as equal
to each other. Some people will undoubtedly be
fulfilled in marriage, but others find fulfilment in
singleness.*

Margaret Evening

The solid wooden door opens, releasing a surge
of welcoming warm air into the cold winter's
night. We step down off the street, straight into
the living room of a delightful, compact, eighteenth-
century terrace house, only 50 metres from the church
we have just left. Several friends are already relaxing in
the veteran armchairs. The ceiling stoops above the
ancient-looking black beams that barely clear our heads.
The room is tastefully decorated; class on a budget.
Carefully chosen, framed, modern prints hang from the
walls. A first-rate recording of Vivaldi is playing
quietly to anyone and no one. Books, records and CDs
spill off the shelves. Well-worn rugs of uncertain
maturity murmur welcome yet again. A long, low, solid
table bisects the room. Already it is full of speciality
cheeses, mainly of French origin, hot bread rolls,

23

straight from the oven, scones, jams and a giant metal teapot with a wooden handle.

Our host is David, a gentle man precise of word and warm of heart. It is his custom every Sunday evening to invite a sundry selection of worshippers to enjoy his hospitality. Laughter, social gossip, deep philosophical reflection and the week's news ebb and flow for an hour or so. Some are regular guests, others require introductions. The nurse sitting uncomfortably on a floor cushion is using all her pastoral skills to draw the newcomer on the wooden chair in the corner into the conversation. He seems happier just to be there than to participate. Despite her best efforts he withdraws tortoise-like into an island of silence amidst the sea of sound. Another rap on the door knocker, guests come in and coats, scarves and gloves come off. A secondary school teacher is relegated to the foot of the stairs, as now the bodies well outnumber proper places to sit. Everyone fits in this feast of simple fare and priceless love: older, younger, the serious and the frivolous, the weak and the apparently strong. No qualification is necessary to attend.

Many present are single. They particularly welcome this inclusive atmosphere. The warm and open relationships meet a real need in their lives. David understands. He is a bachelor, aged 38, a systems programmer at the Open University. He graduated from Cambridge University with a first-class degree in Theoretical Physics before gaining his Ph.D. An active Christian for twenty years, he has given himself to youth work in the church, and through summer camps. He is discreetly open about his desire to be married. But, as he put it, he has not yet met someone who is 'attractive, available and agreeable'. Past relationships have not led anywhere.

In his measured manner, David is gently critical of Christian views of singleness. Subtleties matter to him. It is people's attitudes that wound. 'I'm surprised you have not settled down yet.' As a mature man he does not fit into people's expectations. Singleness is supposed to be a transitory state, not an enduring one. He feels let down by the church's superficial teaching on sex and the single person: 'suppress it and wait'. 'What do you do *now*?' he asks.

* * *

One of the quieter members of the throng is Joyce. With her evasive eyes, hidden behind her glasses, and her nervous disposition she is easily identified as one of society's less fortunate individuals. She suffers from epilepsy. It hindered her education. When not playing truant, she was the one who was the butt of every joke, the odd one out, the one the penultimate in the class triumphed over.

Joyce is brave. It is no fun being a punch bag, but she bounces back. Her disability has made work difficult to find. She cannot concentrate for long. It takes her great effort to achieve, but achieve she does.

A fast-flowing society dedicated to making maximum profit has no room for the weak. Most of her short adult life she has worked in publicly subsidised employment for those with special needs. Even there she has been taken advantage of by unscrupulous individuals. Feeling rejected by her own family, with few friends and even fewer prospects, she came to the brink of a nervous breakdown.

Homeless, she was given a temporary place in a hostel run by a Christian, who introduced her to the church. There she found a friend, another young single lady who had seen God repair her own broken life, a person who really cared. This was someone Joyce could talk with, who accepted her as she was beneath her exterior. Theirs was a mutual friendship. Soon afterwards Joyce prayed with her friend to commit her life to Christ.

Joyce's experience of men has not been good. She has every reason to distrust them. Under current circumstances she prefers to be single. Even in the housing co-operative where she now lives, some of the other residents, especially the men, seem to enjoy making her life fraught.

She says, 'I'm happy being single most of the time, but it's lonely. I do a lot of writing and needlework, so I'm busy most evenings. I've got mates at work and friends at church but no one includes me in on their evenings out. On odd occasions I'm invited to Sunday dinner. I feel left out, that I'm not good enough, or wanted. In an ideal world I'd like a boyfriend who would take "no" for an answer, is easy to talk to, would be understanding of my silent moods, and not get annoyed with me. I would like him to be a Christian like me.'

I'm sure God is thrilled with Joyce. She is making the most of her life. She knows something of His love for her. All the Joyces of the world deserve our greatest respect.

* * *

Sally cannot make the Sunday night get-togethers regularly. She is 'forty-something' with two teenage children who are developing their own social lives and often need ferrying around. At the weekends the children visit their father and his new family, and Sally uses her freedom to socialise. It is refreshing to be free of the responsibility of others just for a short while.

Sally is another single person who demands respect but has not always received it. She was brought up in a Christian family that was one of the pillars of a large evangelical church, well known and well loved. After university she married a fine young Christian It seemed an ideal relationship. She gave up her career to bring up their children, although both she and her husband kept up their church commitments.

Then this started to go badly wrong. His behaviour became increasingly intolerable. She reacted. They fought. Bad became worse, and to the horror of both family and church they separated. Sally's family remained loyal and sympathetic despite this shock. The church reaction was far less helpful. A weaker Christian would probably have lost her faith, faced with so much criticism and judgementalism. It compounded her intense feelings of guilt. Those she thought to be dear friends, and some were, ostracised her. She felt the lion's share of the blame heaped upon her. The less that people knew, the quicker they were to condemn. The church was unable to cope with the situation. She stopped attending. It was the darkest hour, and the night was to be too long.

After eleven years the marriage ended in divorce. Sally kept custody of her children. Sensibly, she moved to a new town. She resumed her career to provide for her young children and started attending a new church. For years she steadfastly resisted pressure to become a member. The hurt inflicted in the previous church was too deep to make such a commitment. It took a total of six years and a lot of love and counselling from the ministry team before that was possible.

Recently she has been forced to think about the possibility of remarriage, which she believes is permitted by Scripture. She wants to be married and believes it would be best for herself and her children. Although the church accepts her personally, she feels that its life is built around the two-parent family, and does not always recognise the particular needs of one-parent families.

Sally has a resilience to adversity that can make her intolerant of trifles, whilst deeply sympathetic to those in real need. Her laugh is care-worn, but there is a new sparkle in her eyes. It is so good that she has rediscovered the love of God for her.

* * *

Becky admits she is struggling with her singleness. She is an attractive and lively 27 year old, and would dearly love to be a wife and mother. She has been a committed Christian since childhood, and joined the church as a teenager. She left home to do her nursing training; a very lonely time, she recalls. She now lives on her own in a typical suburban 'semi' with two cats for company.

What she finds hard is that many of her friends are now married. She says, 'Friendships change and fade. In many ways, being single I have to make an extra effort to talk to people and make relationships.'

With no children of her own, Becky likes to enjoy those of her friends. Recently, at the conclusion of a service, there was a time of prayer for women who could not have children. The problem was, that the desires of single women wanting children were not mentioned. Becky felt very hurt that her pain, and the pain of many others, was overlooked.

She also believes that she is discriminated against at work. 'My pay will only be increased when I have gained more of life's experiences, i.e. marriage and family!'

For Becky, her singleness is a temporary phase of life. A time of waiting, to be made the most of, but only tolerable if it has the happy ending she longs for. That is likely, but there may be more emotional ups and downs and days of unfulfilled longing first.

* * *

James is the centre of attention. Perched on the arm of David's well-worn settee, he is eagerly describing his recent experiences as an aid worker in Africa. With a tell-tale tan, and a rather dramatic haircut of uncertain quality, it is his first Sunday back home from his latest assignment.

He is an intensely spiritual man in his mid-twenties, earnest to the extreme and with a refreshing naïve otherworldliness. Maybe living and working amongst the poorest of the poor breeds a communion with God that is not so easily understood in middle-class suburban England.

He has taken a conscious decision to postpone marriage for the present. His heart is in serving God amongst those in great physical and spiritual need. Being single is a positive advantage, particularly in the team situation to which he will soon return. The decision has not been easy. He would like to be married

29

eventually, and has not been short of admirers. Despite bouts of loneliness, his mind is made up. Marriage is not for now.

'I'm at peace about being single. I am fairly certain to be married one day, and that feeling takes away any pressure. I realise that at the very time I am becoming ready for marriage, I am narrowing my chances of finding a wife. But I see singleness in terms of the positive advantages it brings, rather than the loneliness or stigma. I'm content. I can wait.' James applauds churches that give a positive encouragement to family life: 'It is a great witness in today's crumbling society. However, such churches often misunderstand single people, seeing them as either incomplete, or lacking in some way.'

He highlights a common problem. 'There is inevitably gossip whenever I talk to a single woman.' Apart from this he feels his own church caters well for single people, certainly better than some he knows.

Another question has bothered him deeply. 'I've been asked, "If you don't have a girlfriend, do you have a boyfriend?" It offends me more than I'd ever thought.'

There is an element of the 'old school' about James. He has a pioneering spirit, and an exemplary commitment to world mission. He has taken seriously the challenge of Scripture, to put first the Kingdom of God. He is investing his singleness in the service of his Lord.

* * *

One of the regular 'Sunday nighters' is Ginny. She is very happily married, in her thirties, with two immaculate (in appearance, if not always in behaviour!)

children. However, she is always on her own at church. Her husband is not a Christian. She is one of the so-called 'church singles'. 'Jesus is the number one in my life. The most important *thing* in my life is meaningless to the most important *person* in my life. I cannot discuss it with him, ask his advice, or pray with him. I long to do these things. He is a very good husband. In most areas of life there are no difficulties being married to a non-Christian. I am generally happy and content, but at times it feels lonely, frustrating or empty.' She pinpoints a practical difficulty: 'I want to tithe, but my husband sees this as folly when we don't have enough for ourselves.' She works part-time as a domestic cleaner and gives what she can out of her earnings.

'Being married to a non-Christian is a very public sin,' she says. 'If I had been committing adultery and then repented, no one would ever know or even question me about it. The problem is other people's attitudes. "Why doesn't your husband come to church?" They assume that either I became a Christian after we got married, or that I deliberately disobeyed God by marrying him. Neither is true, and both are hurtful. The church I grew up in did not teach about Christians being unequally yoked with non-Christians. I was only eighteen when we married. I acted in ignorance. When I realised I had not acted according to God's will I confessed my sin and received His forgiveness. I studied the Bible and discovered that we should not separate or divorce. I don't want to!'

'The thing that most alienates me is when people assume that I must be deeply unhappy. The only thing I would change about my husband is his lack of faith. He is a very interesting person, a loving husband, gentle

31

father and good provider. It's just that he is not yet a Christian.'

* * *

Rachel enjoyed a good laugh at James's hair. She is a qualified hairdresser. For the present she can only work part-time from her council house as she has a young toddler to bring up on her own.

A rebel without a cause in her teens, she left school as soon as she could. Regretting this later, she attended night school to gain some qualifications.

When she found herself unexpectedly pregnant and uncertain about having an abortion, she turned to the church for help. One of the ministers, a single lady, opened her own home to Rachel and provided support in word and deed. During the pregnancy, Rachel committed her life to the Lord.

Whatever she does is done with enthusiasm. Christianity, if it was real, was to be taken seriously. Her life changed dramatically, and instantly, even if maturity has taken a little longer to arrive. She has learned to cope with the limitations and frustrations of single motherhood. Her beautiful daughter is now an outgoing toddler and shows every sign of being loved. The Bible is an important book to Rachel, needing to be studied and obeyed. One of her latest moves is to enrol in a Bible correspondence course because she desires to learn more than she gets on Sundays.

She does not know if she wants to marry. 'I'm indifferent. I do not see singleness as a condition I need to be cured of. The Lord may want to keep me single for a number of years. Then again, He may not. Either way I'm neither happy, nor unhappy about it. The choice is not mine but God's. It's not my life to do what

I want with. Personally, I now see that this life is very short in relation to eternity. Therefore, is it so important that everything is hunky-dory now?'

* * *

Two friends from the church who prefer each other's company rather than the boisterous atmosphere of David's open home are Grace and Alice. Both are retired and now live alone. Both combine the dignity, and the deliberateness, of their age with a love of life and practical involvement in the church. Both have had difficult times in their lives.

In 1980, Grace lost her husband after 28 years of marriage. He had been seriously ill for most of the previous twenty years and had consequently been in and out of work. Grace worked to support the family as well as bring up her three children and look after an invalid husband. They moved home several times as he managed to find work. Soon after they moved to Milton Keynes, he died.

Grace's faith sustained her throughout. For most of her life she worshipped in an exclusive branch of the church which is distinguished by some unusual beliefs. After her bereavement she left the church as she realised that there was more to being a Christian than she had been taught. She was renewed in her faith.

All her children married and moved away. She is proud of being a grandmother many times over, and she has been able to offer long-term support to her children and their families as they too have experienced illness and difficulty. Grace is long-suffering and administers rebuke, when necessary, with great gentleness. She is conscious that she is growing old and that with this her health is deteriorating. She says, 'I enjoy my new found independence, but miss the companionship. It is not really loneliness, but being unable immediately to share problems within the family and to receive support. Most of the time I'm happy, but get rather low when feeling unwell or when I'm exhausted, after helping the family. At times, I feel they take me for granted, although at heart I know they don't.'

She finds church very family and couple orientated. In her typically sympathetic style, she explains, 'It's very difficult for them to understand something they haven't experienced, but I do think they should try a little harder.'

Most people who meet Alice assume that she too is a widow. Not all older singles are. Alice does not disabuse them, it is not necessary. In fact she had to divorce her husband after his long-running infidelity. Both her children are married with children of their own.

Ideally, Alice would prefer to be married, but is 'basically happy . . . at times somewhat lonely. One has to get out and meet people, join things. It's no good staying at home feeling sorry for oneself. My son and daughter-in-law are very loving and welcoming, but I find the lack of someone my own age to talk things over with, a little difficult. I am happy to accept the situation though. At least I can make my own decisions!'

* * *

Although names and certain details have been changed, at their own request, everything else is fact. Every one is different; they have different perspectives on life. They are just a handful of the single people attending the church. It was difficult to choose who to ask to take part. I am deeply grateful for their contributions. For many it was hard to express their true feelings, to recount past and present pain, as well as their hopes for the future. Their words speak for themselves.

Although these pen portraits are not intended to represent every type of single person, their diversity is apparent—not-yet married, never married, divorced, widowed, single parent and church single. Even when drawn from the confines of one suburban British church, they are different, educationally, economically and socially, as well as in age, gender and housing. No one from an ethnic minority is included. I had intended to ask a Nigerian student friend to give his perspective. However, during the time this book was in preparation, his family back home arranged his marriage to someone just completing her studies. With his approval the two families made all the arrangements, the dowry was paid and she flew to Britain to be his wife. His own presence at the wedding was not necessary!

There is no such category as 'the singles'. There is no valid stereotype which is appropriate to cover the diversity that exists within our churches. These are not 'singles', they are people. That is why the church must act on the issue of singleness. It is primarily about people, real people who constitute one-third of all adults attending our churches.

2

Singleness in Modern Society

Sex is the mysticism of materialism and the only possible religion in a materialistic society.[1]

Malcolm Muggeridge

It is a woman's business to get married as soon as possible, and a man's to keep unmarried as long as he can.

George Bernard Shaw

There are more single adults living in Britain today than ever before. This alone is a reason for Christians to be concerned about issues of singleness. Single people are not to be measured simply by statistics. Each is a unique individual. Analysis of figures and trends cannot be a substitute for caring for people. However, if we only look at the immediate we are prone to miss the 'big picture'. A strategy is essential for the long term if our day-to-day involvement with single people is to be effective. We need to understand what is happening in our society.

The current social changes affecting the singles population in the UK have largely gone unobserved by the church. Such changes normally happen slowly and may be subject to reversal. Major trends are often only observable after a period of time. Those caught up in them are frequently unaware of the fact. They only see their personal situation, not the broader picture. It is necessary to put the changes into their historical and geographical context to understand them. Their significance will then be apparent and the need for action obvious.

The Historical Perspective

The twentieth century has seen dramatic changes to everyday life in the developed world. These changes have only recently begun to be seen in other parts of the world as Western influence spreads. Changes to patterns of marriage and family life within Britain can be seen within the context of Europe as a whole. The nations of the continent fall into four broad groups: the largely Protestant nations of the north, including Britain; western and central Europe; the predominantly Roman Catholic countries bordering the Mediterranean Sea; and the nations of eastern Europe previously under Communist government. Social trends have often followed the lead of the Scandinavian countries and the example of the United States of America. To get an idea of what may happen in the future in one country it is helpful to view the general picture and to compare that country with similar nations.

In the conservative countries of eastern Europe the first part of the century was marked by very high marriage rates. The population married young. In the West a greater proportion of the population never married, although this was still a small percentage of the total. The average age at which people married was older than in the east. Between the two world wars this average fell in all parts of the continent. In northern and western Europe this trend for younger and younger first marriages continued after the Second World War until around 1970. At the same time the numbers of people marrying at some time during their life also rose to record levels. Over 90% of European women could expect to marry before the age of 50. In eastern Europe rates went as high as 97%.[2]

In Great Britain the proportion of the total population who were married rose from 33.1% in 1901 to a peak of 50.8% in 1971. Before the First World War about 19% of British women and 13% of British men never married. One result of the enormous loss of life in that war was a shortage of males of marriageable age despite the natural surplus of males at birth (104 males to 100 females). Since 1945 the excess of males to females in the 15 to 44 age group has been restored. In 1971 there were 1,376 bachelors for every 1,000 spinsters in that age group; an excess of eligible males that was not apparent amongst church-goers.[3]

As the first chapter illustrated, single adults are a diverse group. They can be broadly separated into:

- young adults, likely to marry in the future
- thirty and forty-somethings, less likely to marry
- mature never-married singles
- those separated and divorced
- widows and widowers
- single parents.

In Britain all these categories, other than mature never-married females, are growing fast.

In 1990 in England and Wales there were approximately 19.5 million men and 20.9 million women over sixteen. 31% of men (6.0 million) and 23% of women (4.8 million) had never married; 3.7% (720,000) of men and 14% (3.0 million) of women were widowed; 5.6% (1.1 million) of men and 6.6% (1.4 million) of women were divorced. Out of 40 million people over the legal age for marriage, 17 million were single people of all different types.[4]

The Last Twenty Years

A very significant change has taken place since the start of the 1970s. Since then, fewer people have been marrying and the age at which they do has risen steadily. The precise turning point varied from country to country, with Sweden leading the way, whilst in the more socially conservative countries of Spain, Portugal, Greece and eastern Europe, the changes were delayed until the 1980s. By 1980 only 69% of all Swedish women married before their fiftieth birthday. In eastern Europe marriage rates fell only slightly but it is likely that the recent political changes in these countries will accelerate the trend. Sweden also has the highest average age for first marriages. In 1988 the average for women was 27.9 years compared to 24.6 years for England and Wales. The average age of a British man first marrying in 1989 was 27.7 years. The British figure had jumped from 21.4 in 1971 and is continuing to rise. The four groups of European nations still have their traditional similarities, as Figure 1 on p. 41 shows, but all are experiencing the tendency to postpone marriage.

Fig. 1 Total period first marriage rate and mean age at first marriage for women, 1988, selected countries of Europe.

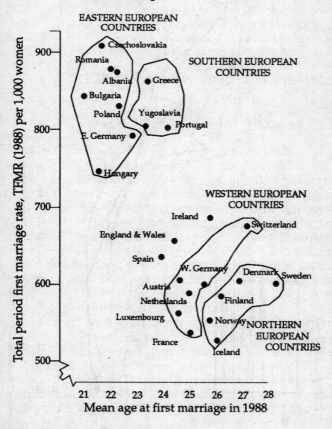

Source: *Population Trends* 69, Autumn 1992, OPCS

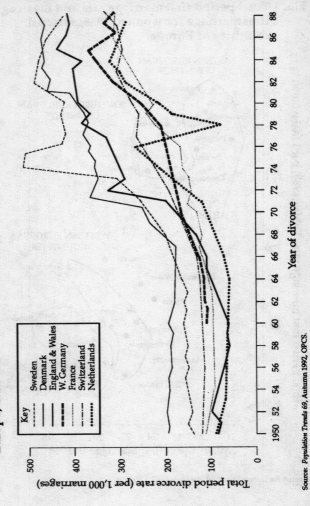

Fig. 2 Total period divorce rate for selected countries of Northern and Western Europe, 1950–88

Source: *Population Trends 69*, Autumn 1992, OPCS.

42

Fig. 3 Total period divorce rate in 1988 and average annual increase in this measure, 1965–88

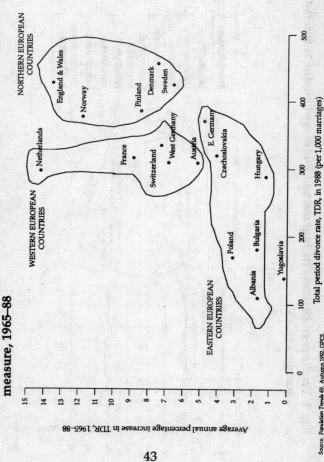

Total period divorce rate, TDR, in 1988 (per 1,000 marriages)

NORTHERN EUROPEAN COUNTRIES

WESTERN EUROPEAN COUNTRIES

EASTERN EUROPEAN COUNTRIES

England & Wales
Norway
Finland
Denmark
Sweden

Netherlands
France
Switzerland
West Germany
Austria

E. Germany
Czechoslovakia
Hungary

Poland
Albania
Bulgaria
Yugoslavia

Average annual percentage increase in TDR, 1965–88

Source: *Population Trends* 69, Autumn 1992, OPCS.

43

Fig. 4 Marriage and divorce in England and Wales, by type and compared to EC partners

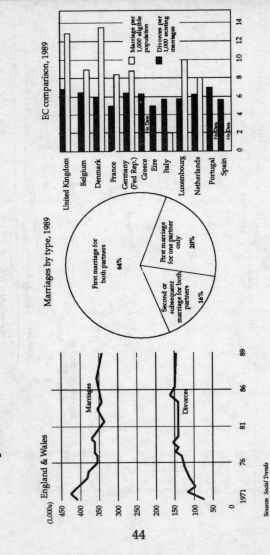

EC comparison, 1989

☐ Marriage per 1,000 eligible population
■ Divorces per 1,000 existing marriages

United Kingdom
Belgium
Denmark
France
Germany (Fed Rep.)
Greece
Eire
Italy
Luxembourg
Netherlands
Portugal
Spain

Marriages by type, 1989

First marriage for both partners 64%

First marriage for one partner only 20%

Second or subsequent marriage for both partners 16%

England & Wales
(1,000s)

Marriages

Divorce

Source: Social Trends

44

Fig. 5 Percentage of all women who were cohabiting, by age, selected countries

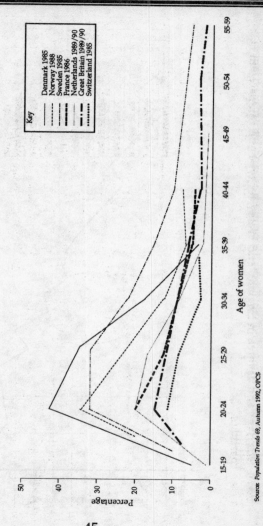

Key
Denmark 1985
Norway 1988
Sweden 1985
France 1986
Netherlands 1989/90
Great Britain 1989/90
Switzerland 1985

Age of women

Percentage

Source: *Population Trends* 69, Autumn 1992, OPCS

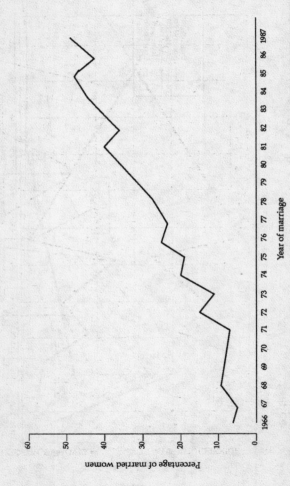

Fig. 6 Proportion of women cohabiting with future husband before marriage: Britain

Source: Population Trends, HMSO

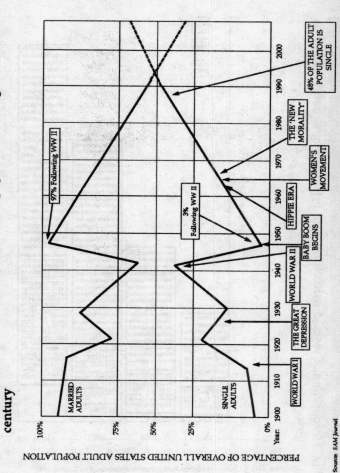

Fig. 7 Development of America's single adult population during the twentieth century

PERCENTAGE OF OVERALL UNITED STATES ADULT POPULATION

Year: 1900 1910 1920 1930 1940 1950 1960 1970 1980 1990 2000

100% 75% 50% 25% 0%

MARRIED ADULTS

SINGLE ADULTS

97% Following WW II

3% Following WW II

48% OF THE ADULT POPULATION IS SINGLE

THE 'NEW MORALITY'

WOMEN'S MOVEMENT

HIPPIE ERA

BABY BOOM BEGINS

WORLD WAR II

THE GREAT DEPRESSION

WORLD WAR I

Source: *SAM Journal*

47

Fig. 8 Ageing trends among the elderly: Britain

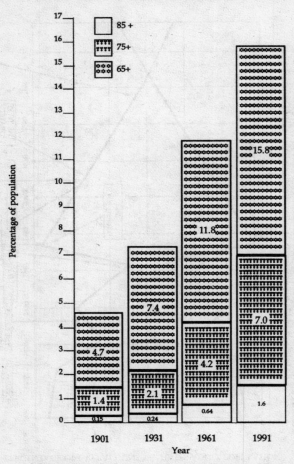

Source: *Family Change and Future Policy*, Family Policy Studies Centre, 1990.

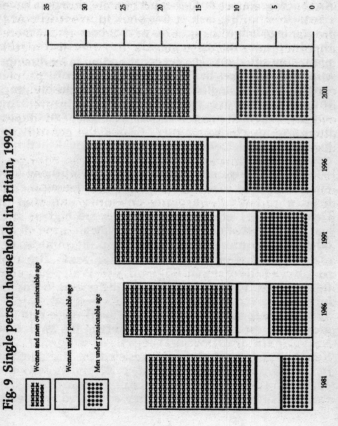

Fig. 9 Single person households in Britain, 1992

Percentage of all households

Women and men over pensionable age

Women under pensionable age

Men under pensionable age

Source: DOE / SDD / Mintel

Divorce

Divorce makes a major contribution to the growth in the numbers of single adults across Europe. The figures are affected by changing legislation in each country; as it has become easier and cheaper, so the numbers have risen. It is not the task of this book to investigate how far the legislative changes may have been the cause of the increase, or may merely have reflected the prevailing situation. However, it is remarkable how the number of divorces has grown during the century. Both world wars resulted in a surge in divorces in the years following, before rates returned to something approaching their pre-war levels. In England and Wales there was an average of only 593 divorces annually for the period 1901 to 1910. By 1989 the annual total had risen to 150,872.[5]

In 1950 England and Wales had one of the lowest rates of divorce in western Europe, well below that of France and West Germany and only half that of Denmark. In 1988 Britain had the second highest rate, just less than that of the Danes and way ahead of all the other EC countries. In the north European countries the rate of increase of divorce has now slowed. The total number of divorces in England and Wales has also fallen since 1989, although it is still one of Europe's highest.

Figure 2 on p. 42 shows how the divorce rate has grown in western Europe. It was only in the 1960s that Italy, Spain and Portugal legalised divorce. The Republic of Ireland alone has resisted the pressure for more liberal laws. Figure 3 on p. 43 shows how the divorce rate for different groups of countries has changed since 1965 and how they compared with each other in 1988. It shows that at the prevailing rates 10–30% of recent east European marriages will end in divorce, compared to one-third of those in western Europe and up to half in northern Europe. Also, marriages are not lasting so long. The average length of a marriage in England and Wales ending in divorce was 11.5 years in 1963 but by 1989 this had fallen to 9.7 years.

It is estimated that, at current rates, 37% of all marriages in England and Wales will end in divorce. The *proportion* of British divorcees remarrying is falling although the *total number* doing so is still rising. In 1974, 64,080 (22%) divorced men and 61,660 (14%) women remarried. In 1989 the respective figures were 84,035 (8%) men and 81,702 (6%) women. Increased levels of co-habitation are a major cause of the drop in remarriage rates. Co-habitation also accounts for the longer period of time between divorce and remarriage. Second marriages are less stable than first marriages, with a significantly greater failure rate. Figure 4 on p. 44 gives detailed comparisons.

Co-habitation

One of the most significant factors to emerge in the last twenty years has been the growth of co-habiting, a couple living together within a sexual relationship without being legally married. Few European statistics are available. The practice has grown rapidly to become of social significance only recently. Government agencies have not attempted to monitor the number until the last few years. It is obviously difficult to know when a couple are in fact co-habiting, as they may still have separate homes, or may not be agreed about the nature of their relationship, which normally evolves over time. As with other trends the Swedes and Danes have led the way within Europe.

Figure 5 on p. 45 shows the co-habitation rates of some European countries. As the last ten years have seen an enormous increase in the popularity of living together *before* and increasingly *without* marriage, it is significant that the proportion of British couples co-habiting in 1989/90 (which was greater than five years earlier) still fell far below that of the three Nordic nations (Sweden, Denmark and Norway). It is also apparent that most women co-habiting are under 35. In Sweden, where co-habitation has been common for longer, there are much higher rates of older couples living together. This is likely to be the experience of other European countries in the future.

In Britain in 1971 only 7% of single women co-habited before marriage: by 1987 almost half did (see Figure 6 on p. 46). Unofficial estimates now put this at 70%. In 1987 an estimated 1.8 million people, 12% of all unmarried men and 14% of all unmarried women aged 16–59, were co-habiting. In the south-east and East Anglia the rate rose to 16%, around twice that for Wales (7.8%) and Scotland (9.4%).[6] The practice has become widely socially acceptable. Most recent data from the UK Office of Population Censuses and Surveys indicates that in England and Wales couples co-habiting before marriage are 50% more likely to divorce, within five years, than those who do not.[7] With increased levels of pre-marital co-habitations, the future prospect of many marrying today is statistically bleak.

The USA Experience

If the situation in Europe is surprising, the situation in the United States is more startling. As Figure 7 on p. 47 shows, almost half of all adults in America are now single. Divorce is a major factor. In 1920, one in seven marriages ended in divorce, by 1960 it was one in four, in 1972 one in three, and in 1977 one in two. In 1985 only 54.3% of all marriages were first marriages for both partners, 23.4% were remarriage for both, and 22.3% where one partner was remarrying, whether divorced or widowed. Up to two-thirds of all American remarriages after divorce result in another divorce.[8]

Widows and Widowers

The populations of most Western countries are also increasing in average age. Between 1961 and 1988 the life expectancy of a British woman increased from 73.8 to 78 years and for a man, from 67.9 to 72.4 years. The percentage of elderly people has been growing rapidly. In 1901 the UK had only 1.7 million over-65s; by 1988 there were 8.8 million. (See Figure 8 on p. 48.) The UK now has over half a million people aged 85 and over, compared to a mere 57,000 in 1901. In 1987 only 45% of the over-65s lived with their spouse, 36% lived alone and 19% with relatives or in other circumstances. 61% of all women over 80 live alone.[9]

The fact that a large number of the over-65s are widows and widowers has also swelled the proportion of single adults in society. In several west European countries the total population is now shrinking as birth rates have fallen to unprecedented lows. The population is no longer replacing itself. In both absolute and percentage terms the number of elderly single people is likely to rise well into the twenty-first century, posing serious problems for governments, churches and families alike.

Single Parents

In Britain today 17% of all families are headed by a single parent—the highest percentage in the world. There are 2.1 million children living in these families. In 1971 only 8.4% (65,000) of all births were to unmarried mothers, but this has risen to 28.3% (200,000) in 1990. 80% of mothers under twenty years were unmarried, although this does not necessarily mean they will be single parents. It is increasingly common for such births to be registered in the name of both parents; in 1966, 38.3% of all births outside marriage were so registered, compared to over 70% in 1990.[10]

Lone parents may never have married, divorced or been widowed. In 1988, of the 16% of British families with only one parent:

- 1% had a lone father
- 5% had a never-married mother
- 1% had a widowed mother
- 6% had a divorced mother
- 3% had a separated mother.

Single parent families are not evenly distributed throughout the country. As they are more likely to be

54

poor, they are more common in areas of cheaper housing, such as the inner city. In 1981 in inner London 26.6% of all families were single parented. This may also reflect the tendency for London and the south-east to have more liberal social attitudes than other parts of the UK.

Single Person Households

Not only are there more single people than ever before in the UK, but more are choosing to live alone. Only one in four British households now consists of a traditional nuclear family of two parents living with their children; this is now less than the proportion of homes occupied by a single adult.

In 1951, 10% of households in England and Wales had only one adult. This had risen to 17% by 1971 and to 25% by 1984. The figure is expected to rise to 40% by the end of the century (including single parent households). In 1992 this was a total of 6 million dwellings and it is expected to be approximately 8 million by AD 2000. Older people are the largest single group. Some 3.7 million single households are occupied by someone over 65.[11] Single parents and unmarried adults choosing to live alone constitute the remainder. See Figure 9 on p. 49.

As affluence has increased so more people have been able to afford this option of owning their own home, denied to earlier generations. It is increasingly common for British young people, especially those from a middle-class background, to take out a mortgage on a home before contemplating marriage. In a more mobile society where people move home in search of work, away from their family home, it is an inevitable process.

Why Have the Numbers of Single People Grown?

The various statistics and charts track the growth of the singles population. But why have numbers grown? The reasons are political and economic as well as sociological. Divorce has grown through changes in legislation, alongside changes in social attitudes. In previous centuries divorce was largely limited to the rich and famous—only they could afford it. Divorce still causes financial hardship for many, but changes to the law have limited responsibilities, enabling people of all social and economic groups to divorce. The law, generally, only reflects the will of the people.

Marriage is increasingly seen as a necessary convention to regulate relationships for as long as two people consent to it, instead of a lifelong commitment by two people before God and the community, and is for convenience; the elements of pleasure and gain are stressed before sacrifice and service of partner and family. Marriage may be delayed or dissolved to fit in with the rest of life. For most women, career and marriage now mesh together, rather than follow each other. If marriage, or bearing children, are likely to harm progress at work, with the financial security and personal satisfaction it brings, then many choose to forsake them.

The breakdown of traditional communities, where successive generations lived in the same streets and intermarried with neighbouring families, has had an effect on the number of single adults. In those close-knit families children only left the parental home when marrying. Parents were not only concerned, but sought to influence their children in the choice of a partner. The model of a happy, stable family life was a positive spur to the next generation to seek and expect the same for themselves. If this ideal was not universal it was certainly more true in previous centuries than today. Individualism has replaced the idea of the family as the dominant factor in most people's judgement.

Many young people today have seen the inside of an unattractive model of the family and found it wanting. Whether it is because of a so-called 'broken home', as a result of domestic violence or child abuse, or just a family home full of tension and strife, they are refusing to make the same binding commitments as their parents. However short-sighted it may seem, the looser relationships common today appear to offer an easier and less painful way out if things go wrong. Better the insecurity than to be 'trapped' in a loveless marriage or to be savaged by a brutal divorce.

Attitudes to Singleness

The number of single adults throughout the Western world has grown dramatically in the last twenty years. But have attitudes changed? It is easier to quote statistics than to monitor attitudes.

Marriage remains popular in the UK. Britain has the highest rate of marriage, as well as the highest divorce rate, of the countries of the EC.

Society is still very couple orientated. Social invitations may no longer be to 'Mr & Mrs . . . ' but to 'so and so' and 'partner'; whether attending weddings, meals or parties, the single person without a partner is still an embarrassment.

The effect of the 'sexual revolution' of the 1960s has been profound and long-lasting. The convenience and relative certainty of the contraceptive pill, the easy access to abortion, the decriminalisation of homosexuality and the application of a widespread rejection of Christian religion to the area of personal morals combined to break the sexual expectations of single people. It is not that young single people did not commit fornication before but not so many did, it was normally furtively done, at a higher risk of causing pregnancy and was generally accepted as 'wrong'. Historically, singleness and celibacy were, at least nominally, synonymous. In French, 'Je suis célibataire' means 'I am single'; today no one thinks it means 'I am a virgin.'

Confusion often exists over modern usage of the word 'celibate'. Its traditional meaning (and the one still given in dictionaries) is of a never-married person who is therefore a virgin. In popular usage today, however, it merely means a temporary abstinence from sexual relations without reference to a person's current marital status or history. It is in this modern sense that many of the following quotes, and some textual references elsewhere in this book, use the word 'celibate'.

The '60s overturned biblical and traditional morality. As with most revolutions it happened because it was a reaction to a situation that needed to change. From a Christian perspective it cannot simply be dismissed as a total disaster. We can never be seen to condone hypocrisy and double standards. Freedom is a word which is compatible with the gospel even if selfishness is not. Most young women would not want to turn the clock back to the time when the *only* option was early marriage, followed quickly by children and the routine of domestic life.

The possibility of a fulfilled single life has always existed. For a Christian little has changed. To be single means abstinence from all forms of sexual intercourse, both homosexual and heterosexual. Mental purity and emotional responsibilities in relationships with others have always been tough challenges.

If someone rejects, actively or passively, Christian morality, they can expect to be both single and sexually active. To our modern mind 'no sex' seems an awful loss; this is perceived to be the big negative of traditional singleness. Now, one can have one's cake and eat it. It is this mentality which makes life difficult for Christian singles today. If they are celibate they are part of a strange minority, often deliberately misunderstood and parodied rather than respected.

The advent of AIDS has had little effect on the sexual behaviour of heterosexual singles. They often regard themselves as 'low risk' and would follow 'safer sex' advice rather than abstain from intercourse. Those who have moderated their behaviour do not do so because of a Damascus road conversion to Christian morality, but to 'look after number one'. Sadly it does not herald a new dawn of Christian values. The church has a long way to go to convince society that God's laws are the only basis for a long-lasting, stable, just and peaceful community.

The Media

The British press recognises the growing numbers of singles in society. It regularly runs features on single people and their life styles. Most take for granted the prevailing attitude to singleness considered above. The *Guardian* journalist, Edie Jarolim, typically expressed this attitude in an article on singleness:

> I've been married, single, in between, and I think the single times have been the best . . . I liked and loved my husband . . . but as soon as we crossed that legal threshold, I felt trapped . . . I'd like to have sex occasionally but it always seems to be attached to angst of some sort . . . I've found that sex is a lot like caffeine—an addiction you can kick.[12]

Of prejudice against singles in a couples orientated society Marcus Berkmann of the *Daily Mail* wrote: 'Once valued for their independence of spirit and carefree existence, singles are now the new social lepers: barred from couple-dominated dinner parties, humiliated at company social functions, subject to probing questions from suspicious aunts.'[13]

Regional writer, Valerie Webster, summed up her feelings:

> Most women who want to marry can do so . . . if they don't meet the right man with whom to contemplate a shared lifetime, they need no longer remain virgins unless they make a moral decision to do so . . . Living alone, whether from

choice or necessity, has its good and bad points, and personally I'd choose it in preference to a stressful, conflict-torn family life any day . . . [Living alone] has an image of being pathetic, dangerous and eccentric . . . and [making one] an object of slightly derisive pity among the ones who think they'll avoid it.[14]

Sally Ann Lason of the *Daily Mail* wrote of discrimination against singles: 'Supermarkets are obviously designed by married people for married people. If you fancy some mangetout for your supper . . . you must buy enough for a week . . . [Packs of vegetables] sit on the shelf glowering at you, society's silent reproach for your failure to find a partner.'[15]

In the *Daily Telegraph*, Lesley Garner pointed to the dangers:

A nation of solitaries, blissfully selfish and set in their increasingly eccentric ways, is not a nation brimming with neighbourliness or social concern . . . I know many people who live alone and lead rich, full lives, but, in their more thoughtful moments, all admit what hard work it can be . . . There is a danger that your own company [may] become preferable to anyone else's and so inhibit the formation of close relationships with others.[16]

Angela Hughes, of marketing specialists Mintel, commented on their survey of British singles: 'Our main finding was the positive attitude of those living alone, emphasising the freedom and sense of achieving in coping, rather than loneliness or lack of security. Those who have never been married have the most positive attitude.'[17]

In a *Company* feature entitled 'Single-minded', legal secretary Jo Collier (aged 23), is quoted as saying:

> People look at a single woman and assume, not that she's alone out of choice, but that it's a consequence of her having no one to go out with. Worst of all, I can't honestly say that when I see a woman sitting on her own I don't look twice. That's conditioning for you![18]

Times writer, Liz Hodgkinson, author of *Sex is Not Compulsory*, goes against the general trend by advocating celibacy. She writes:

> Sex experts try to make us believe that without frequent sex we will become unbearably frustrated and repressed. In fact the reverse may be true. Many people discover that their physical health improves during a time of voluntary celibacy . . . Although a life of celibacy is popularly imagined to be one of misery, deprivation and continual frustration and repression, it can be the very opposite and provide a wonderful opportunity to get to know yourself, understand who you are and what your real purpose is in life. It can also allow you to develop hitherto undiscovered talents. The idea that sex increases human happiness started only with Freud . . . [19]

Repeated media focus on the issue has given rise

to suggestions that singleness is only a concept for the 'chattering classes'. Life for the so-called working class is more pragmatic: people have jobs (if they are lucky), not careers. Family and community are more important than the individual.

Singleness in Ethnic Minorities

In the Afro-Caribbean community two main subgroups have emerged: the traditional Caribbean, which generally accepts a biblical world view and in which the church is still an important influence, and the secularised (and often politicised) black community. West Indian society is largely matriarchal. It is more orientated to the wider family than its Western counterparts. Tensions often occur between young people and their elders. Marriage is still very much the norm but frequently a non-Christian couple will not marry until after the birth of their first child. There is often liberal behaviour despite conservative moral beliefs—the difference is seen as being 'cultural' rather than hypocrisy. The macho male image dominates. Rastafarianism which thrived on urban alienation is now being replaced by Black Islam; this represents another challenge to Christian values. In the black-led churches in Britain there is a severe shortage of men, which creates real difficulties for black Christian women in their late twenties and thirties seeking a partner.

The Asian community in the West adheres largely to its traditional cultural patterns. Marriage is a parental or community responsibility. Adult singleness is largely an unknown concept. If someone is unmarried something is 'wrong'. It reflects badly on the family.

There is intense pressure to marry. Sometimes an older man (30+) will marry a younger bride who, if necessary, will be found for him from a suitable family back in Asia. Many young Muslim women are denied educational opportunities because of their marriage prospects. Marriage is expected to be in line with caste expectations (i.e. someone from the same stratum of society). Christian converts from Hindu, Muslim or Sikh families will frequently come under intense pressure to marry someone from their original religion in the hope that the convert will revert to their original faith. A significant minority of Asian young people revolt against the pressure of arranged marriages, wanting the freedom of their Western peers and creating great tension within their community.

Homosexuality

If a mature single man lives on his own for a period of time and does not have a girlfriend, it is likely that his neighbours will start wondering, 'Is he gay?' If he has men friends to stay overnight the neighbourhood can quickly confirm its erroneous conclusions!

Recent research in both the UK and the USA has shown that only 2% of men say they have engaged in homosexual acts at any time. The gay community, which has consistently maintained that one in ten men has a homosexual orientation, disputes the findings. It is likely that the gay community is much smaller than has been generally accepted—particularly by the media. A quarter of a century after the decriminalisation of homosexual acts between consenting adults over 21, British society as a whole still does not know how to react to gays and lesbians. The gay community itself is split over whether to be a distinct subculture or to integrate into mainstream society. At the risk of oversimplification, four common attitudes can be identified:

1. *Closet acceptability.* This is in the old public school upper-middle-class tradition which for many led on to a career in the church or the army. Such people were often accepted in positions of power within the establishment which turned its blind eye to 'private' behaviour. Occasionally, someone like Quentin Crisp would challenge this silence.

2. *Animosity.* Homophobia is alive and well. Real hatred and fear is easily unearthed. Extreme right-wing political groups, sections of the press and many older people have a non-intellectual, emotional, negative reaction. This instinctive response may show in discrimination, prejudice or even violence. 'Queer-bashing' is still likely to recur periodically.

3. *Advocacy.* Not only the gay and lesbian communities but also many civil libertarians and minority rights campaigners normally associated with the political left support homosexual equality (e.g. inheritance laws, parental rights, etc.) and positive discrimination. The demise of the 'looney left' of the British Labour Party has meant less media attention but its supporters are still active. The call to 'come out' will continue. The spread of AIDS and HIV has undoubtedly weakened the political and social momentum

for change, whilst evoking sympathy for those who are suffering.

4. *Ambiguity*. Perhaps the majority of people remain ambiguous on the issue. Intellectually, they accept homosexuality as an alternative to heterosexuality. Emotionally, they are repulsed by the idea of sleeping with someone of the same sex. Socially, they can accept the discreet gay but dislike public displays of affection by two men or two women. They feel protective towards their own family and children. They would prefer not to talk about the subject, for fear of their internal contradictions.

Large sections of the gay community feel rejected by Christians. Many Christians with a homosexual background face the difficult challenge of living a celibate life because they now believe homosexual practice is wrong, but find the idea of heterosexual intercourse foreign to them. Their opposition to homosexual activity can often lead to conflict with their non-Christian counterparts, who may resent even sympathetic Christian attempts to reach out to them with the love of Christ.

Summary

This survey of singleness in society has attempted to demonstrate the size and diversity of the singles communities today. This very diversity can obscure the significance of their presence. The idea of discrimination against single people on the grounds of their aloneness is laughable, and yet it happens. Knowing the facts is only the starting point. Governments have had to recognise the significance of the predicted growth in the number of single people because of its likely impact on housing, social services, pensions and population growth. The church can appear to be more tardy.

---

1 Quoted in Wroe, Martin, ed., *God: What the Critics Say* (London: Spire, 1992).

2 Most of the European statistics are taken from *Population Trends 69, 1992*, Office of Population Censuses and Surveys (HMSO). The comparisons are with data for England and Wales only, not for the whole UK.

3 See *Annual Abstract of Statistics*, HMSO.

4 *Projections of the Population by Marital Status, 1985–2025, England and Wales*, HMSO.

5 OPCS. Quoted in Cornes, A., *Divorce and Remarriage* (London: Hodder & Stoughton, 1993) p. 9.

6 *Population Trends 58, 1989*, OPCS.

7 *Population Trends 68, 1992*, OPCS.

8 US Bureau of the Census. Quoted in Cornes, op. cit., p. 10.

9 *Population Trends 66, 1991*, OPCS and Kiernan K. and Wicks M., *Family Change and Future Policy*, 1990. Quoted in Care Fact Sheet, February 1992.

10 *Population Trends 66, 1991*.

11 *Social Trends 20*, HMSO and 'Single Person Households—Single Living, Diverse Lifestyles 1992', Mintel International Group, London as quoted in *The Times*, 15 September 1992.

12 *Guardian*, 20 June 1991.

13 *Daily Mail*, 23 January 1990.

14 *Milton Keynes Mirror*, June 1984.

15 *Daily Mail*, 17 September 1992.

[16] *Daily Telegraph,* 16 September 1992.

[17] Quoted in the *Daily Mail,* 15 September 1992.

[18] *Company,* December 1988.

[19] *The Times,* 19 January 1993.

3

The Situation in the Church

*Of Archbishop Lang: 'in the loneliness of his bachelor
life his great need was not for friends, of whom he had
plenty, any more than it was for work, of which he had
too much. It was for that old, simple, human thing—
someone in daily nearness to love.'*

Quoted in M. Evening, *Who Walk Alone*

The world is changing, but has the church
changed? In 1992 two important surveys
attempted to uncover what the current situation
is within the British church. Singularly Significant
surveyed member churches of the Evangelical Alliance,
to discover the numbers and breakdown of their single
adults. Administry, the agency set up to improve the
quality of church administration, surveyed its members
to see what progress had been made on twenty
recommendations drawn up by a Singularly Significant
consultation in 1987. It published its findings in a
resource paper for local churches.[1] It was primarily
concerned with structures and the pastoral implications.
Both surveys provide us with invaluable insights.

Nearly 300 churches representing 37,000 adults
took part in the Evangelical Alliance survey. A total of
34.8% of those over eighteen attending are single, a
finding which came as a surprise to many of the
churches themselves! This percentage is only a little less

69

than the percentage of single adults in the population as a whole. The churches were categorised according to their type of locality. See Figure 1.

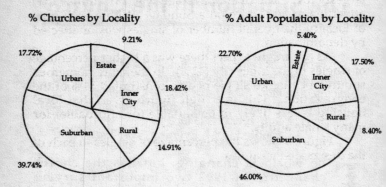

% Churches by Locality   % Adult Population by Locality

Fig. 1 Churches were categorised by locality

Figure 2 shows the average size of the congregation by locality.

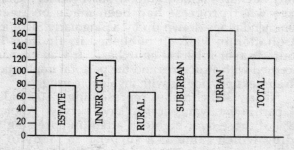

Fig. 2 Average congregation

The average congregation ranged from 74 in rural churches to 167 amongst urban churches. Independent churches were on average smallest (102) and Anglican largest (184). The overall average was 131 adults (18+) attending at least once on a Sunday. Within each type of locality the overall number of singles was unaffected by denomination.

As one might expect there was a higher percentage of singles in the inner city (42%). In the more numerous suburban churches single people constituted 31% of the congregation. This is a high figure given that local housing is less likely to be suitable (or affordable) for many single adults.

Figure 3 shows the percentage of singles in each of the designated localities.

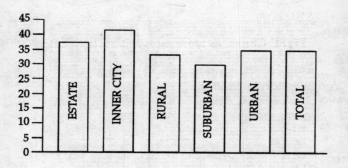

Fig. 3 Percentage of singles per congregation

When all the singles were placed into categories some interesting distinctions emerged. An average of 63% had never married, 3.7% were separated, 9.4% were divorced and 24% were widowed. Widows and widowers were most common amongst the estates and least common in the inner cities. Never-marrieds were slightly less common in estates but constituted almost two-thirds of the total singles.

Almost 70% of singles in the inner city in independent churches, which includes new (or house) churches, were never-marrieds, but only 16% were widowed. In the Church of England only 55% were never married and 33% were widows or widowers. (See Figure 4.) Churches attract a greater percentage of widows and widowers than in the population as a whole, but fewer divorcees and, unsurprisingly, very few co-habitees—less than 1% overall and spread very thinly across a range of churches. Three-quarters had no one in this category.

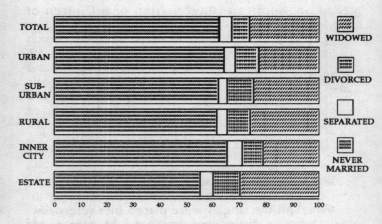

Fig. 4 Singles by category

Churches are divided as to how to regard co-habitees. 58% regard them as singles, presumably because legally they are. 29% treat them as married, presumably because they are living as if they are. Those churches with co-habitees attending are more likely to regard them as married than those churches without such people regularly attending. The survey highlights a difficult issue which could become a more common problem in the future. However, at present co-habitees shun the church. An estimated 15% of all adults aged under 59 are currently co-habiting. This is a very large segment of the population that the church does not appear to be reaching.

More common are married people whose spouses do not attend church. The so-called 'church singles' are almost 9% of the total surveyed. They are more likely to attend an Anglican congregation or a Church of Scotland (11%) than an independent fellowship (6%).

Encouragingly, 40% of all single adults in church are aged under 30, 60% under 45, and 27% over 60. Inner-city churches have the most young singles and fewest over-60s. The survey revealed some dramatic differences between the age profiles of single men and women, as Figure 5 on p. 74 shows. Over half (53%) of single men are under 30, three-quarters (76%) under 45. A third of all single women (33%) are under 30 and 42% under 45. Single women over 60 outnumber their male counterparts by six to one and are one-third of all single women in church. They form a greater percentage of a rural church or parish church. Only 41% of singles in the Anglican churches surveyed were under 30, but 65% of all singles in the independent churches were in this age group. By contrast, in the independents only 10% of their singles were aged over 60, less than half the proportion attending the Church of England (21%).

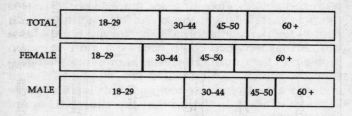

Fig. 5 Percentage singles by age group

It is no surprise that women outnumber men by more than two to one (68% : 32%); however, this disguises some major variations. Amongst the under-30s the difference is much less dramatic (56% : 44%) or 1.3 women to every man. If you live in a rural area the ratio is almost equal (1.1 : 1). As age increases so does the dominance of single women over single men. In the 45–59 age band the ratio rapidly climbs to 3 : 1. (See Figure 6 on p. 75.) There are a lot of single men under 30 in evangelical churches, although still not as many as single women. It is the lack of single men over 45 that gives the overall imbalance. This imbalance is more pronounced in Baptist (70% : 30%) and Anglican (71% : 29%) churches than in the other denominations.

Reasons for single people joining or leaving a church are evenly divided between marriage, work, study, retirement and house prices, except amongst suburban churches where work was given as the dominant reason.

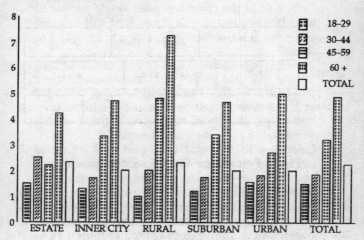

Fig. 6 Single females to males ratio

The survey also sought to find out how the church's existing life and ministry met the needs of its singles population. The key findings were:

• More than half the churches surveyed integrated single people into their leadership structures, although this was more common in the inner city than in the rural areas where two-thirds do not have any singles involved. The numbers involved are quite low, however:

single people make up only 26% of the church leaders but are 35% of the church membership.

- Only half of the churches used single people to lead house groups. Of those that did women were much more likely than men to be asked to do so.
- Nearly three-quarters of churches (72%) had single people involved in leading their children's work. The overwhelming majority of these were single women. 75% of churches had single leaders of youth work; these were a very even mix of male and female.
- Only one in five churches had any activities organised by or for single people themselves, or offered any regular, organised practical help for them.
- Few churches feel that single people make a significant contribution to the ministry of preaching in the church (21%), although two-thirds believe single people play a significant contribution to the pastoral care of the congregation.
- Just over half (51%) recognised that single people make excellent baby-sitters!
- The most commonly recognised feeling of single people themselves was that of loneliness, although this was expressed in many different ways. Other issues mentioned were lack of self-worth, responsibilities for elderly relatives, transport, sex before marriage, need for practical help, dating non-Christians and bereavement/separation support.
- Asked to assess how well they felt their church

was doing in meeting the needs of single people, just over half (54%) said 'adequately', a quarter 'poorly' or worse and one in five 'well' or 'very well'. It must be stressed this is the leaders' own assessment—we do not know if the singles in the church share the same view.

'Single-minded', the Administry survey, looked at issues more qualitatively. It found little if any evidence of progress towards implementation of the twenty recommendations drawn up by *Singularly Significant* in 1987. These recommendations form Appendix A of this book. Administry encouraged the churches to let their singles speak for themselves. This revealed a great deal of emotion and hurt lying just beneath the surface.

About half the churches had never had a serious discussion about singleness. A third had never taught on related issues such as celibacy. The report exposed that some singles feel that they are seen as second-class citizens, by both the leadership and the members of their church. Much personal evidence is given of unthinking discrimination and insensitivity, although one correspondent did not feel actively discriminated against, just forgotten! The churches did not generally have a policy excluding single people from leadership of house groups, but many still do not have any single leaders. Until it was brought to their attention some had not even realised this!

The question about 'family services' provoked some strong reactions, primarily about the title rather than content of these meetings. 'All-age worship' is the preferred alternative. Churches reported that some of their singles will deliberately stay away from the service as they 'feel' excluded because they are not part of a family as popularly defined. They also dislike the term 'church family'. Other singles, mainly women, avoid Mothering Sunday because it is too sensitive and can appear to value a woman only if she is a mother.

'Single-minded' reports that most churches say that groups specifically for singles are not always the answer. Groups which are age-related or interest-based are more likely to succeed.

Defining the goals, vision, structures and leadership of any group is vital. Many churches have groups for the 18–30 age group, which are, too often, perceived as all that is necessary to meet the needs of single people. Within larger churches there are now, often, enough single people of different types, such as single parents and older singles, to justify meeting together. All-age singles groups are rare but do exist. Amongst the helpful ideas in the report are a 'bereavement group' and a discussion group on 'sexuality and the single male'. It is wonderful that at least one church has not just recognised the need to talk about celibacy, but is helping its men to live a pure life. A common emphasis was on providing a social programme rather than another meeting. This appears to meet a genuine need. Such groups may live for only a short time before they need to be reborn. Their membership is often transitory. Special events are an alternative to the group and can work well, although they miss the opportunity for building long-term friendships.

Other problems highlighted were:

- Holidays. They are often difficult times for many single Christians. Bank holiday outings, special Christmas dinners, a holiday week for single mums, and relief for single carers were good ideas mentioned in response.

- Christians with unconverted partners. Their negative experiences included misunderstanding, over-zealous evangelism of their partner and insensitive preaching, but these were balanced by low-key support, encouragement and prayer groups for the 'church singles'.
- A lack of teaching on singleness (but not on marriage, and family life) and failure to use sermon illustrations and applications relevant to single people.
- House groups. Openness and honesty about relationships and sexuality in mixed small groups is difficult. Single people may find it difficult to speak openly about their true feelings.
- Youth groups normally do teach about relationships and sexuality, but this may be the only place these subjects are taught with reference to single people.

This report exposes the weakness of many churches, and draws into question the self-assessment made by the church leaders in the Singularly Significant survey, which is quoted above. The anecdotal evidence from single people themselves suggests that more churches are doing 'poorly' than 'adequately' or 'well'. It seems that most churches have little concept of what is needed. It is a case of widespread ignorance rather than deliberate neglect.

The American Church

A comparison may be drawn with attitudes of church leaders in the USA. There, 88% of all large churches in a recent survey have established Singles Adult Ministry (SAM) programmes.[2] One-third of these churches have a full-time single adult pastor. Interest in SAM programmes is growing. 67% of churches rate it more important now than five years ago. They also report that the number of single adults attending is increasing. Almost three quarters (72%) had more than 50 people enrolled in their singles programme. One other finding of note was an apparent link between interest in overseas Christian mission and the percentage of singles attending: the more singles present, the greater the degree of interest in missions.

Another survey of smaller American churches revealed that they attract fewer single adults and are much less likely to run their own singles ministry.[3] A quarter currently link with neighbouring churches to provide this. More than half felt a programme specifically for singles was needed. The obstacles to doing so were a lack of numbers, too wide an age range, and the present integration of single people into the existing structure of the congregation making targeting difficult. The accompanying report stressed the need for a different approach in the smaller church with a small singles group, building on the natural advantages of its size, rather than focusing on its disadvantages. These advantages are intimacy, ease of communication and organisation, and doing one thing well.

Other evidence from the USA is less encouraging. Only 15% of American single adults felt the church was sensitive to their needs whilst 46% of families responded positively to the same question.[4] Most American churches are not attractive to the vast majority of the singles in their society.

An issue regularly raised in churches with a singles ministry is a lack of resources. It is a low priority when the church budget is set and suffers accordingly. The senior pastor may not be closely in touch with the programme because he is overstretched. As in the UK there is a similar bias in the USA towards married people in leadership. Julia Duin, an American and author of *Sex and the Single Christian*,[5] complained in a recent article that in the church we are separated according to marital status and that the vast majority of leadership positions are occupied by the married. In 1990, even in USA church single groups 61% of leaders were married. She rightly asks why it does not work the other way round when appointing a senior pastor.

Summary

In terms of its constituents, the British church is changing. As the proportion of single adults in the community is rising, so the same is true in the church. However, there are significant differences: the church has more older singles and young never-marrieds, but fewer men and almost no co-habitees. Its structures, attitudes and awareness of singles issues has not changed accordingly. Few yet recognise the demographic shift and its implications.

Exclusive 'family-ism' is still the order of the day. Concepts such as 'family church' and 'family services' need to be revised. In Scripture the church is *not* described as a family but 'the household of God'

(Eph. 2:19 AV), a much broader term implying the wider, rather than the nuclear, family complete with servants, guests and any other resident. The household of God is *all* who dwell under the same roof—not just a part.

Many single people do feel treated as second-class within our churches. This runs directly counter to the New Testament emphasis on all being equal before God. In fact, Scripture teaches that those on the outside fringes of society, such as widows and orphans, should be especially welcome in the church. Paul teaches that single people can be of extra benefit in leadership and service, and yet we display a bias against single leaders.

There is an urgent need for action and a change of attitude to match the reality of the situation in the church today. The church is people and a whole category of people is feeling neglected. We must quickly move to put this right before the pain and loss become more widespread than they already are.

---

[1]'Single-minded', Administry Resource Paper 92:4 November 1992, published by Administry, 69 Sandridge Road, St Albans, Herts, AL1 4AG.

[2]*Single Adult Ministries (SAM) Journal* 69, Vol. 7, No. 3, January 1990.

[3]*Single Adult Ministries (SAM) Journal* 91 & 92, Vol. 9, Nos. 5 & 6, March/April 1992.

[4]Barna Research Group, Glendale CA. Quoted in *SAM Journal* 89, Vol. 9, No. 3, January 1992.

[5]London: Marshall Pickering, 1990.

4

A Theology of Singleness

For a member of the Body of Christ, marriage is no longer a necessity or a duty, for man is no longer alone as Adam was; he is the friend of Christ, he lives in the communion of saints, and he is indwelt by the Holy Spirit.

Max Thurian

The Bible must be the basis of our understanding of singleness. Approaching the subject with an open mind, however, may be difficult. If we conceive of singleness as a problem to be solved or as the privilege of a spiritual élite, we are likely to reach biased conclusions. Our culture inevitably shapes our thinking, but it may be necessary for the Word of God to reshape our perception.

Sadly, none of the books on singleness I have read contain an adequate investigation of what Scripture has to say about the subject.[1] Most start from a personal perspective. They are often laced with Bible references to many different related subjects, such as relationships and loneliness, but are very light when dealing with singleness itself. In the local church sermons on the subject are at a premium. If you hear one, tape it—it is a real collector's item!

Why is there this reluctance to deal with singleness from Scripture? Some are under the mistaken impression that there is nothing substantial in the Good Book about it. After all, was not singleness virtually unknown in ancient Israel?

Others have discovered 1 Corinthians chapter 7 but do not know how to handle it. For many singles struggling with their situation it tells them all they do not want to know. They do not regard being single as better than marrying, as Paul seems to say (v. 8). His teaching would appear to appeal to only a minority of highly motivated individuals and those with a masochistic desire to deny themselves the thing they most want in life.

The subject is often ignored in the local church because those responsible for the teaching programme often fail to appreciate how important it is. This is despite the evident popularity of teaching on the subjects of marriage and the family. Alas, the logical extension of such a series to cover the circumstances of the rest of the congregation is rarely considered.

We have space for but a brief treatment of the subject. If it stimulates others to study the subject for teaching or writing a more comprehensive article or even a whole book, it will have achieved a major goal.

THE OLD TESTAMENT

At first sight it may appear that the Old Testament has almost nothing to say on the subject. Certainly there is no passage that gives an exhaustive treatment. What it does say must be gleaned. It is certainly set against a culture in which celibacy was rare although, as we shall see, not unknown.

Creation and the Fall

God created man as a perfect individual in His own image (Gen. 1:26–7). God could not improve on His design. Man's fundamental identity as a living being was 'good'. He was the pinnacle of creation. As Adam before the fall was acceptable to God on his own so, after redemption, any individual today is acceptable to Him. He was not judged by who his family were or what job he did. These were important but followed after God's affirmation of his identity.

Up to this point the unfailing comment of God is that what He saw was either 'good' (Gen. 1:4, 10, 12, 18, 21, 25) or after the creation of mankind 'very good' (Gen. 1:31). Adam was a physical being formed out of 'the dust of the ground' and a spiritual being receiving 'the breath of life' from God Himself (Gen. 2:7). He had a superb environment (vv. 8–14) and had work to do (v. 15).

But something was missing. God makes a surprising comment, in contrast to His previous responses, 'It is not good for the man to be alone' (v. 18a). Human beings have a social dimension. We need company. This is a primary statement about community which must be properly considered before progressing to the following sentence which introduces the concept of marriage. It is a principle for all mankind, whether single or married, that 'It is not good to be alone'. Ecclesiastes 4:9–12 amplifies the thought: 'Two are better than one . . . If one falls down, his friend can help him up . . . if two lie down together, they will keep warm . . . Though one may be overpowered, two can defend themselves.' This scripture is too often quoted

85

as if it refers exclusively to marriage, rather than relationships in general, which is its context. We all need good relationships because that is part of our nature.

The primary, rather than only, provision of God to meet this need is in marriage. God continues, 'I will make a helper suitable for him' (Gen. 2:8b). In one Jewish commentary on v. 19, as the animals parade in pairs before Adam he sadly comments, 'Everything has its partner but I have no partner.'[2] No animal is suitable so woman is created as a partner for man. She is equally in the image of God (Gen. 1:27). They are complementary to each other, made for sexual union with each other (Gen. 2:23–4). Both male and female sexuality is God-given and therefore good. Sexuality is part of our distinctive identity as individuals. It is neither to be ignored nor despised; in their original state Adam and Eve were naked together without any shame (v. 25). Single Christians today face the challenge to enjoy their sexuality without sexual intercourse as its natural outlet.

The two major consequences of the fall (Gen. 3), death and the disruption of relationships, are both directly relevant to singleness. Without the entry of sin into the world there would be no widows or divorcees. The pain of unfulfilled desires for a partner is inconceivable in a perfect world. The fall affected relationships between the sexes (v. 16). There is a release of (animal?) desire in the woman not previously present, which will distort normal relations. Female friends speak of that time in their monthly cycle when they can experience an intense desire for sex with a man and of the great pain that it is never met. The balance between Adam and Eve in the 'suitable partnership' of

Genesis 2 is replaced by 'he will rule over you' (v. 16).
Work for Adam now becomes labour. We can see
the roots of the common contemporary tension
between work and relationships. Too many single
people, of both sexes, today face difficult decisions
between marriage and career. It is arguable that
the fall did not create singleness but did put the pain
into it.

The Community

For God's covenant people life was in the context of the
community and the community was built on the family.
The family was a much wider unit than we know today.
Three or four generations might live under one roof or
certainly in the same village. It would be unthinkable
under normal circumstances for an unmarried man, let
alone a woman, to set up home on their own. If a
previously married member of the family became single
again, most commonly when a woman was widowed,
they were to be provided for by their relatives. If no one
could do this or those who could did not do so, then
God instructed that the wider community should. This
was primarily through the 'second tithe' where those in
need were allowed to glean the harvest (Deut. 14:28–9;
25:5–10; Ps. 68:5–6).

A young man could expect to marry before
reaching twenty and a woman was usually younger
still. It was therefore normal for a man to be a
grandfather whilst still in his thirties and a great-
grandfather before reaching 60! Marriage was the
responsibility of the parents or the wider family if they
were not alive. To a Jewish family this was a sacred

duty. It was a disgrace if they failed to do this. God had decreed, 'Be fruitful, and multiply' (Gen. 1:28 AV) and, 'It is not good for the man to be alone' (Gen. 2:18). The earth was to be 'filled' and each generation had the responsibility to continue the growth in population. Without a clear concept of life after death, the early Jews also saw descendants as the only way to ensure the survival of their name.

The sorry story of Jephthah illustrates this sense of shame. He rashly promised to sacrifice the first thing he encountered on his return home from a great military victory. This was his virgin daughter. She says, 'But grant me this one request . . . Give me two months to roam the hills and weep with my friends, because I will never marry' (Judg. 11:37). She and her friends went and wept together for the duration until the vow was executed.

The rabbis disputed the meaning of 'be fruitful'. Shammai said it meant a man must have at least two sons. Hillel countered it meant he should have a son and a daughter because God created both male and female.[3] He also argued that for a man not to marry was to diminish the likeness of God in the world since mankind is made in the image of God (Gen. 1:26–7).

An early Jewish commentary on Genesis 2 states, 'Whoever has no wife lives without good, without help, without joy, without blessing, without atonement, even without welfare and without life.'[4] On Genesis 5:1–2 it adds, 'He (i.e. an unmarried man) is not even a whole man, for the Scripture said he blessed them, and called their name Man.' Consequently few people were given the option to remain unmarried.

But there were exceptions. It was a rabbi's solemn

duty to marry. One, Simon ben Azzai (c. AD 100), taught, 'A man who does not marry is like a man who sheds blood, for he has as good as slain his own posterity.' And yet he himself did not marry. Asked about this contradiction between his teaching and his practice he responded, 'What can I do? I am in love with the Law. The population of the world can be kept up by others.'[5] There are other examples of rabbis, who although married, abstained from sexual relations with their wives for prolonged periods to give themselves whole-heartedly to study the Law. This was considered the only legitimate reason to postpone marriage. However, this was merely a delay, not a substitute.

The Law prohibited sex before marriage. If a husband found after the wedding that his bride was not a virgin, she was to be stoned to death (Deut. 22:20–1). If a man raped an engaged virgin he was to be put to death; if she did not resist she too was guilty of fornication and condemned to death (Deut. 22:23–5). If an unmarried couple were caught having sex and the woman was not engaged to someone else, the man was to marry her and pay a dowry. He was not allowed to divorce her (Deut. 22:28–9).

For a woman there was no career other than marriage. Most were mothers whilst still teenagers. If her parents could not find a suitable partner, once she reached adulthood, the Law went as far as to suggest that a man 'free his slave and give him to her rather than let her remain longer unmarried.'[6] If a divorced woman or widow was rejected by her relatives the only economic alternative was prostitution. The provisions of the Law were to prevent this occurring.

Wisdom and Poetic Literature

The emphasis on the community in earlier Jewish writings is balanced by a greater stress on the individual in the later books of 'Wisdom'. Issues of everyday life are considered from the individual's perspective. Personal moral and spiritual development are common themes.

Proverbs deals with domestic and spiritual life alongside each other. Human friendship is important, e.g. 'There is a friend who sticks closer than a brother' (Prov. 18:24). Suffering and loneliness are questions discussed in Job and Ecclesiastes with which the modern reader can identify.

In the Psalms God is on the side of the oppressed, as elsewhere in Scripture. Psalm 68 pictures God taking up the cause of the orphan and the widow (v. 5). He even 'makes a home for the lonely' (v. 6 NASB).

The Song of Songs graphically depicts male and female sexuality and desire. It is appropriate material for teaching single people about the mysteries of love and relationships as well as for deepening the understanding of married couples for what has already taken place.

The Prophets

Most commentators on the Old Testament are understandably wary of placing much emphasis on the examples given by the lives of key characters as opposed to their teaching. Indeed it is difficult to relate the apparently eccentric lives of the prophets in particular to modern church life in prosperous western

Europe. But to ignore their lives is a mistake. Often their message was strongly demonstrated by the particulars of their calling.

Hosea's disastrous marriage is the most dramatic example of a prophetic message pictured in personal circumstances. He became a single servant of God, separate from his adulterous wife, to demonstrate the sorrow in the heart of God over the backsliding of His covenant people. He was but one of the prophets who, contrary to normal practice, were called to remain single.

Jeremiah was commanded never to marry (Jer. 16:2). Disaster loomed. Families would be devastated by war, disease and famine (vv. 2–3). Bodies of loved ones would lie unburied (v. 4). Mourners would suffer alone and uncomforted(v. 7). Even the usual rejoicing at weddings would be absent (v. 9). All this was a curse that Jeremiah's singleness personified.

Ezekiel was a widower for much of his ministry. When his wife dies he is instructed not to mourn in the usual manner (Ezek. 24:15–18). This is also a sign of God's judgement and the imminent destruction of the temple (v. 21). God sums up the situation, 'So you will be a sign to them, and they will know that I am the Lord' (v. 27b).

Of the other prophets we know little or nothing of their marital status. Samuel was married. Elijah lived alone for much of his recorded life, lodging with others or with his trainees (1 Kgs. 17:3, 5, 19; 18:1; 19:3–4, 15, 21). Both Daniel and Jonah may have been single but we cannot be sure. Nehemiah may have been a eunuch because of his office in the Persian court prior to his return with the exiles, although this may not have necessitated castration. There is no record of him having a family. It is dangerous to argue from silence, but it is consistent with the lonely and unpopular role of the prophet to suggest that a number of these great men were either single or lived as if single for the duration of their recorded ministry. That this was unusual in Jewish society and even a despised state in the minds of their contemporaries merely adds force to their message, and simultaneously bears testimony to their willingness to suffer in the service of their God.

THE NEW TESTAMENT

Between the Testaments there is some evidence that the hard line on marriage as previously taught in Jewish society had moderated at the fringe. The ascetical Essenes practised celibacy alongside marriage. The historian, Pliny the Elder, finds this strange, describing the sect as, 'remarkable among all other tribes in the whole world, as it has no woman and has renounced all sexual desire'.[7] The Qumran community, which shared many similarities with the Essenes, also encouraged celibacy although for what duration is disputed. The Dead Sea Scrolls speak of those who 'live under a vow of celibacy'. This may be because they regarded themselves as living in something of a state of emergency, awaiting their liberation from the yoke of the Romans. Both groups were marginal although probably influential beyond their numbers. Whether John the Baptist was influenced by either has been the subject of much debate. We have no direct evidence to suggest that John was single, but his ascetic life style has prompted speculation that he also forsook marriage for the sake of his calling.

Jesus the Man

Jesus was a single man. The impact that this must have had is difficult to gauge from the pages of the New Testament. He was careful to distance Himself from the perceived asceticism of John whilst affirming His message (Matt. 11:16–19). Yet His celibacy made Him most unusual for a man of His age. It is possible that His singleness made Him the subject of verbal abuse such as, 'You eunuch', which was a term often used disparagingly.[8]

He was completely human, which means He was a fully sexual male. He displays the full range of emotions including love of friends (John 11:36; 15:15; 19:26). He loved children (Matt. 19:13–15). He knew the pain of going without the security and comfort of home and family (Matt. 19:29). He regarded women as equal at a time when they did not have that status (e.g. Matt. 5:31–2; Luke 7:36–50). He understood the nature of male lust (Matt. 5:28) and taught that these temptations must be dealt with by confronting the evil within (Mark 7:20–3). His own life was without sin (Heb. 4:15).

He freely associated with single people of all different types. An elderly widow, Anna, was one of these privileged by God to witness His dedication (Luke 2:36–7). His best friends, other than His disciples, were Mary, Martha and Lazarus, who all appeared to have been unmarried (John 11:5). Single women, from the lowly ex-prostitute Mary Magdalene (Luke 8:2) and the co-habiting woman at the well (John 4:17–18), to the wealthy Susanna[9] (Luke 8:3), became some of His closer followers.

His mother, Mary, is alone at the time of the crucifixion (John 19:25–7); probably Joseph had died

leaving her a widow. This may help explain Jesus'
particular sympathy for widows. The Jewish law
taught that they should be provided for, but Jesus did
more than this. They were amongst the under-
privileged, their right to natural justice was abused
(Mark 12:40). He sought to lift them to a place of esteem
and respect. Jesus points to them as an object lesson of
sacrificial giving (Mark 12:41–4) and prayer (Luke
18:1–5). He had sympathy for the grieving widow of
Nain, and restored her son to life (Luke 7:11–15). In His
care and concern for widows He set an example for the
church to follow.

The Teaching of Jesus

It was this outstanding person to whom the Pharisees
came with one of their double-edged questions, 'Is it
lawful for a man to divorce his wife for any and every
reason?' (Matt. 19:3). There were two rival views on
divorce. The two rabbis mentioned above, Hillel and
Shammai, taught respectively that a man could divorce
his wife for any marital incompatibility or only for
adultery. The Pharisees sought to suck Jesus into this
dispute to gain grounds to criticise Him whichever side
of the fence He came down on. Was He a dangerous
liberal or a hard-hearted literalist?

Wise to their devices, Jesus refers back to creation
and God's original intent that a man and woman should
be united in marriage for life. This pre-dated the
provision in the Law that they were disputing, thereby
emphasising the positive rather than the negative. 'Why
then,' they asked (v. 7), 'did Moses command that a man
give his wife a certificate of divorce and send her away?'

Jesus' reply is that this concession was only instituted because of the hardness of their hearts.

Having made clear the grounds on which He has based His response—no divorce 'except for marital unfaithfulness' (v. 9)—He then clearly takes a conservative stance more in keeping with the followers of Shammai than his rival. Divorce may therefore be seen in both the original provisions of Deuteronomy 24:1–4 and the teaching of Jesus as a humane response to the failures of sinful mankind to limit the damage already caused. It is a last resort, not an available option for a dissatisfied husband. It is a sadly necessary reason for someone becoming single again.[10]

Three Types of Single People

In this encounter Jesus' teaching thus far has been both profound and vitally important, but by no means revolutionary. His disciples comment (sarcastically, chauvinistically, limply or with mock horror?—the text does not make it clear) that it must be better not to get married at all (Matt. 19:10). Surprisingly, Jesus does not contradict them. He goes on to describe three categories of single people: 'For some are eunuchs because they were born that way; others were made that way by men; and others have renounced marriage because of the kingdom of heaven. The one who can accept this should accept (Greek χωρεω, *choreo*, literally, 'mentally grasp', 'accept and act upon') it' (v. 12).

The first two categories are those recognised by the rabbis: the congenitally deformed who are incapable of sexual relations and those who have been castrated by others. There was a general exclusion of those who had been castrated from the worshipping community of Israel (Deut. 23:1) and a particular ban on men with damaged testicles from becoming priests (Lev. 21:20). The idea of disfiguring a man for any reason was abhorrent to the Jews, although castration was a relatively common practice of many of Israel's neighbours. Priests of some of the fertility cults practised self-mutilation as a sign of their devotion to their god. Royal courts had eunuchs in positions of responsibility although the title did not always imply castration. In Isaiah 56:3–5 there is a promise that in the future eunuchs who kept the Law would be welcomed by the Lord into His people.

The third group is Jesus' own institution. The first two are involuntary, whilst the last is entirely voluntary. The first two are physical states, but there is no suggestion that those who are eunuchs for the Kingdom of God are so for physical reasons. Certain leaders of the early church such as Origen (c. AD 185–254) did interpret this text literally and castrated themselves, but this was exceptional. Origen himself later came to regret his action.

The three categories may be designated:

- congenital—those who cannot marry for physical or psychological reasons
- circumstantial—those who do not marry for social reasons
- choice—those who choose not to marry for spiritual reasons.

It is legitimate to see these as three general groups identified by Jesus which have a wider application today.[11]

By no means do all those born with physical disabilities fit into the first group. The emphasis in Matthew 19:12 is of those unable to consummate marriage. Today there are many more people who cannot contemplate heterosexual union for psychological reasons. Those who have a strong homosexual orientation from their youth are in this position. If they wish to live according to God's law they have no choice but to remain celibate. Some victims of child sex abuse may be so damaged that the thought of physical or emotional intimacy is quite repulsive. Without a measure of healing, through one means or another, marriage remains practically impossible for them.

It is the second category of those who are single, because of circumstances rather than choice, that has grown dramatically in modern times. There are many examples. Perhaps the most common reason expressed by single Christians is that they have never met the right person. For women it is that a suitable man has never asked. For a man it may be the frustration of not being in a position to exercise their traditional prerogative. Increasingly people are putting work before long-term relationships. One of the effects of the feminist movement has been to encourage women to pursue their careers but this has often diminished their marriage prospects. For many Christian women over 30 there are simply too few available Christian men. Caring for elderly or infirm parents may mean the carer losing out on opportunities to meet a partner.

Some 'super-spiritual' Christians believe that all they have to do is pray and God will provide a husband/wife. They never get to meet someone who could be the answer to their prayers. Others may be less 'spiritual', stuck in front of their TVs, but experience the same problem; they never meet a potential partner. Many widows and widowers would like to remarry after due time but only a minority have the opportunity. Finally, there are the growing numbers of divorcees who have been rendered single again because of the end of their marriage. They must have been in Jesus' mind, given the context of His statement.

It is the third category that was so revolutionary in Jesus' own day and so little understood and undervalued in the Protestant tradition today. Twentieth-century Western culture has dramatically reacted against the earlier 'puritanism' which was so embarrassed by human sexuality. This has produced a poisonous cocktail of ideas which has distorted our view of celibacy. It is commonly assumed that anyone from adolescence onwards who is not engaging in sexual intercourse is either unfulfilled or repressed or both! For much of the church's history voluntary celibacy was regarded as a superior status; marriage was for the weak who could not control their basic desires. The sexual act was dirty and an embarrassment, necessary only to perpetuate the human race. Since Freud, life without sex has been deficient and the celibate is to be pitied. The call of Jesus to the single life must be re-examined without either of these unhelpful concepts.

Jesus concludes His remarks with the qualification, 'Let anyone accept this who can' (NRSV). The word translated 'accept' implies the need to understand with a view to implementing the teaching personally. This indicates that this state of celibacy is not only voluntary but a calling. Both marriage and singleness are callings and demanding for anyone who is living by the standards of the Kingdom of God rather than selfish instinct.

Paul in his commentary on this teaching is to add that celibacy is also a spiritual gift, a *charisma* (1 Cor. 7:7). The calling is 'for the sake of the kingdom of heaven'. This is a positive emphasis rather than a negative self-denial. There is a good goal in view. Serving God is an even higher calling than the traditional Jewish responsibility to marry and have children. This is not an emphasis common in modern Christian teaching. It is in keeping with other statements of Jesus which emphasise the priority of serving God, the secondary nature of all else and the prospect of divine rewards for those who give up anything for the sake of the Kingdom (e.g. Matt. 10:34–9; 13:44–6).

Many single people reading this may react that they do not feel called to be single, it is an involuntary state and they do not believe God has given them the spiritual gift to go with it! Such responses probably indicate what a poor job the church has done in teaching and training people for singleness, whether lifelong or temporary, in a society which generally despises celibacy. Few have a vision for the single life style because it has not been presented as a valid and ful-filling option for a Christian. What teaching has been given has often been about how to make the best of a bad job, or survive until a partner eventually arrives.

Marriage in Context

The other major contribution Jesus made to the unfolding understanding of singleness was to put marriage clearly into its proper perspective. He emphasised that in heaven there will be no marriage relationships: 'When the dead rise, they will neither marry nor be given in marriage; they will be like the angels in heaven' (Mark 12:25). His listeners probably found this as difficult to accept as a happily married couple do today. We enter this life single, most have the privilege of being married for a time before at least half the population have the experience of being single again. Then, all of us will be single for the whole of eternity, but able to enjoy unspoiled relationships with all our friends and family who are there. Being united with Christ for ever is even more wonderful than being married now. By showing just how short a time marriage lasts for, in the context of eternity, Jesus helps us to see why singleness is not the negative it is normally made out to be.

He emphasised that the love of God was above all else. Married people must love God more than the members of their own family (Luke 14:26). Those who make following Jesus a priority will be more than adequately compensated by God, now and in eternity (Luke 18:29-30). The cause of the Kingdom of God is paramount—everything else, even those things most precious to us, must be set aside if necessary. Jesus' teaching is not just for the highly dedicated missionary spinster, who has put her heart's unfulfilled desire for marriage behind her to serve God in Africa or Asia, but for every true follower of Jesus. For some, seeking first the Kingdom of God will mean singleness; others will make different sacrifices. Whatever demands our calling makes, the loss is both temporary and relative. There is something in life even more important than marriage. It is worth repeating the much quoted maxim of the missionary martyr, Jim Elliot: 'He is no fool who gives what he cannot keep to gain what he cannot lose.' He understood Jesus' teaching well.

Paul's Instructions to the Corinthians

If Jesus put marriage into its eternal context, the Apostle Paul had a tough job to help the Christians at Corinth put singleness and marriage into their contemporary context.

Corinth was famous for its sexual laxity. In earlier times, the temple of the goddess of Aphrodite had been staffed by a thousand female slaves drawing large numbers of visitors it was their duty to entertain. The Greek word *corinthiazesthai* means 'to fornicate'. It had pretensions to philosophy and letters. It could boast of no great native thinkers or university, but was a market-place of second-hand 'wisdom'. In Paul's day it was 'similar to any other cosmopolitan Roman trade centre, no worse and no better'.[12]

The city was strategically important, intellectually and physically conscious, materially prosperous and morally corrupt. Self-indulgence was the order of the day. It has been said:

> The ideal of the Corinthian was the reckless development of the individual. The man of pleasure surrendering himself to every lust, the merchant making his gain by all and every means, the athlete steeled to every bodily exercise and proud in his physical strength are the true

Corinthian types; in a word, the man who
recognised no superior and no law but his own
desires.[13]

Paul wrote the first letter to the Corinthians in
answer to a series of questions the believers had posed.
(See 1 Cor. 7:1, 25, 8:1 and 12:1.) Some of them had so
reacted to the moral laxity of the city that they embraced
a false asceticism based on the teaching of Greek
philosophers, who believed that the body was
intrinsically evil, and sexual intercourse was only for the
unspiritual. Others felt they could do just what they
liked because the body did not matter. They thought
they could engage in sex with a prostitute because it
only involved their body! (See 1 Cor. 6:12–20.)

In chapter 7, we have the most extensive teaching
about singleness contained in Scripture. Paul is trying
to teach a balanced view of both marriage and celibacy,
in the light of 'the present crisis' (v. 26). The crisis was
probably either local persecution or the ordinary
troubles of life. It could refer to a period of tribulation
prior to the return of Christ (cf. Luke 21:23), but this is
less likely. Certainly Paul was acutely conscious of the
shortness of this life (v. 29) and the temporary nature of
this world (v. 31), and his advice (v. 25 ff.) in the light of
this closely echoes Jesus' emphasis of putting God's
affairs first (v. 32ff.).

Some have suggested that we can ignore this
chapter other than as an illustration of life in the first-
century church, because of Paul's reference to the
circumstances surrounding the church. He believed his
advice was inspired by the Lord (v. 25) and it is clear
that he gave the same teaching to all the other churches

he was in contact with (v. 17). We may be confident, therefore, that what he says is relevant today.

Both to married people seeking to get out of their commitments and to single people seeking to take on those responsibilities, his advice is the same: stay as you are (vv. 8, 10, 12, 26, 40). Paul wants the best for them. He denies that the Corinthians who were married would be better off abstaining from sex. They should enjoy frequent relations—only abstaining for limited periods, mutually agreed, to give themselves to prayer. Paul is highly pragmatic, he recognises that the flagrant immorality all around created a problem that for married people was best met in the natural way (vv. 1–5)! Similarly, if an unmarried person or widow cannot cope with sexual temptation, Paul advises them to get married (v. 9). Very basic but sound advice, appropriate for today.

Paul was not in any way anti-sex. Within marriage it is good. The apostle nowhere encourages people to remain single because sex is sinful or God's second best. One happily married US professor of theology shocked his students by remarking on v. 9, 'There are a lot better things that can be said about marriage than that it is not a sin.'[14] Paul had a high view of marriage which he teaches elsewhere (Eph. 5:22–33). It is not his purpose to expound that in this passage. Here he gives his high estimation of celibacy.

Max Thurian, one of the founders of the Taizé ecumenical community, pledged to poverty, celibacy and obedience, sums up his approach to this chapter: 'It is an exhortation to true Christian marriage for people who avoid it without having received a call to undertake celibacy . . . rather than a panegyric of celibacy and virginity. In this way everything assumes its proper place.'[15]

If a Christian embraces celibacy, for a limited period of time or for their entire life, Paul is concerned that they do it for the right reasons. He believes it is good for many people to do so (vv. 6, 27, 38) but not for the reasons the Corinthians were advocating. This principle remains of vital importance. Single Christians today need a biblical understanding of their own status so that they are able to be positively single rather than unfortunately unmarried.

Paul Himself

Paul wishes that everyone was single like himself (v. 7). It is interesting to speculate what type of single person Paul was. As a Jew, and particularly as a devout Pharisee (Phil. 3:5), it is likely that Paul married as a young man. It is apparent from his travels recorded in the Acts of the Apostles, that he was living as a single man for the duration of his Christian ministry. In 1 Corinthians 9:5–6, he expresses his frustration at the way he and Barnabas are denied the rights given to others. Peter and the other apostles take their wives with them on their travels, Paul and Barnabas do not. J. Jeremias, C. K. Barrett and other commentators believe Paul was a widow.[16] More interesting is F. F. Bruce's suggestion that Paul's wife left him following his conversion. If so, this adds weight to his sympathetic advice in chapter 7 to believers with non-believing partners (vv. 7:12–16).[17] We cannot be sure. The answer does not affect the impact of either his teaching or his example, that to serve his Lord it was best for him to remain single, and that what was best for him was best for others too (v. 8). His emphasis is firmly on the present and the future, not the past.

A Gift of Celibacy?

In verse 7, Paul states a general principle that he repeats elsewhere; every believer receives gifts (χαρισμα, *charisma*) from God. (See Rom. 8:32; 12:6; 1 Cor. 1:7; 12:4–7.) In this context he appears to be thinking of two mutually exclusive alternative states, both of which need God's grace: celibacy and marriage. He has the gift of celibacy (even if he arrived in that state through circumstances he would not have chosen). Most of his readers had the gift of marriage, which they were in danger of abusing. In Romans 12, Paul traces all gifts back to the grace of God. The gifts he quotes (e.g. teaching, encouragement and leadership) are not those received instantly but are those which are developed over an extended time. God's grace enables every believer to exercise his or her gifts, but each individual is responsible for using those gifts to the full. Celibacy is a gift that requires effort: it is not a magic panacea for all ills.

Opportunities must be taken, not ignored. Gifts wither if not used. Effort is necessary to develop them to the full. Just as a marriage demands commitment and hard work to function well, so the gift of celibacy needs to be developed. It does not happen by default but by application. Many singles cause themselves problems because of an unwillingness to accept the proferred grace of God within their current circumstances, preferring to dwell on what might be in the greener grass on the other side. We only receive grace for today, not for tomorrow. This gift of grace does not eliminate the problems, such as sexual temptation, as Paul recognises, but it does promise the strength to meet the challenge. Ignoring the gift of celibacy is the worst of all preparation to receiving the gift of marriage. Equally, ignoring the gift of marriage is potentially fatal to the relationship and no indication of the gift of singleness. Both attitudes are very wrong.

All spiritual gifts are not gifts primarily for the individual but the body as a whole. If a local church has single members they are God's gift to the whole church. Their particular set of gifts, including their singleness, is intended by God to be a vital part of the functioning whole. If either the church or the individual denies, overtly or by default, this gift, inhibiting its use, not just the individual but the whole body will suffer.

Sexual Purity for Singles

Paul reaffirms, by implication throughout this chapter, that sex before marriage is wrong. He makes no concession either to the lax morals of Corinth or to the false asceticism of some in the church. He recognises the force of sexual desire. If it has become an all-consuming inner desire, whether or not it results in unrighteous acts, Paul's advice is to get married (1 Cor. 7:9). He addresses virgins with respect not pity (v. 35). The term here appears to apply to both men and women although in v. 36 it is restricted to women. Some of the Corinthian believers would have been unmarried but not virgins (see 6:9–11). A slave girl probably had little choice if her master wished to take advantage of her. He teaches that purity of the body (6:19–20), the emotions (7:9), the mind (7:37) and the will (7:37) are all important. Paul himself preached a gospel of forgiveness of sin (Eph. 1:7), that Christ cleanses His people of all their impurities (1 Cor. 6:11; Eph. 5:26) and of the need to live sexually pure lives through the power of the Holy Spirit (Eph. 5:3; Gal. 5:16–26). Whatever the past, whatever the environment, sexual purity in the present is required. It was not easy in first-century Corinth; it is not easy today, but God's grace is the same.

Paul's Advice

His advice—as given in 1 Corinthians 7—to various groups of the church may be summarised as follows:

- If you are *married* stay together and enjoy frequent intercourse (vv. 1–6, 10, 27).
- If you *separate from your believing partner* stay unmarried or be reconciled (v. 11). This includes divorcees.
- If you are *married to an unbeliever* stay together, but if the unbelieving partner leaves let them go (vv. 12–16).
- If you are *widowed* stay single, but you are free to marry another Christian especially if you cannot control your passions (vv. 39–40).
- If you are *circumcised* stay that way (v. 18).
- If you are *uncircumcised* stay that way (v. 18).
- If you are *a slave* don't fight against it, but if

you get the opportunity to be emancipated take it (vv. 21–3).

- If you are *a virgin* stay that way, but you are free to marry (vv. 25–8).
- If you are *engaged* get married if you want to, but break the engagement if in your mind you are convinced it is best and you are doing so out of your own free will (vv. 36–8).

In the middle section (vv. 17–24) Paul illustrates his main thesis, 'stay as you are', with reference to three groups—circumcised, uncircumcised and slave—that do not fit into his survey of the different types of marital status. Renegade Jews underwent surgery to reverse their circumcision as happened before the great Maccabean revolt in the second century BC. The very idea was abhorrent to most Jews. Paul's rule for Gentile converts was that they should/need not be circumcised as they were not becoming Jews (see Gal. 2:15–21 and Acts 15). He uses an image of the physically repulsive to illustrate a practice he believed to be spiritually ridiculous. Neither circumcision nor uncircumcision matters any more, so there is no cause for change.

His illustration of the slave is illuminating. 'Be content' is something he says elsewhere (see Phil. 4:11 and cf. 1 Tim. 6:6). This is not, however, a recipe for inaction. It is the proper inner state from which to take action rather than reaction. Hence it is sensible for a slave to take his freedom if it is on offer. Slavery is only for this life, so is not the crucial issue, while being a slave of Christ is (vv. 21–2).

Similarly, marriage is not the most important issue, freedom to serve Christ is. Paul teaches that whether you marry or stay single you do well; it is not an issue of moral principle (except for deliberate, unjustified divorce, v. 11), but a pragmatic issue—what is best under the circumstances. His advice is a mixture of lofty ideals and down-to-earth pragmatism—which is a good combination.

The Advantages of Celibacy

Paul expands on the advantages of celibacy (vv. 32–5). He has already given two:

- We all experience a lot of stress because of the age we live in. Marriage will add to this (v. 26).
- Life is short. Even those who are married are going to have to live as if they are single (vv. 29–31).

He adds:

- He wants them to be free of all concerns. Concern is not a totally negative concept, embracing legitimate responsibilities as well as that which causes anxiety (v. 32a).
- Both unmarried men and unmarried women are free to concentrate on pleasing God. Paul uses the same word for concern in respect of the affairs of God. They are able to be single-minded and holy (vv. 32a–4).
- By contrast a married man has divided responsibilities to please both God and his wife. He must be concerned for matters

temporal as well as matters spiritual (vv. 33–4a). The same applies to a married woman (v. 34b).

He writes equally to men and women alike, showing an enlightenment remarkable for his time. He concludes this section with a graphic image not apparent in most English translations. He literally says 'not to put a halter on you' (v. 35). He is not treating them like captive animals that have to respond to commands, but affirms their freedom to make their own decisions. He is simply concerned to help them come to the best possible decision. For some single people that will be marriage, for others it will be the even better option—remaining single to serve God with undivided attention.

The Implications for Today

Paul's emphasis, that in the light of circumstances singleness is better than marriage, although it is not intrinsically better, sounds strange to twentieth-century Christians. In recent years most evangelical churches have so emphasised marriage that they have lost the balanced biblical perspective. An unquestioned, unbiblical assumption—'marriage is intrinsically better than singleness'—has invaded the general understanding. For the sake of the growing singles population this is an error which must be corrected.

The whole church, not just single people, need to have a biblical understanding and acceptance of singleness. Our current unbiblical perspective results in frequent misunderstandings and imbalanced relationships between church families and church singles. The married population should be positively liberating the singles community to fulfil its God-given mandate of serving the church—not just baby-sitting and Sunday school teaching, to suit the marrieds (although in proportion these activities are fine)—but the *full* range of Christian ministry. With this we must recover a respect for those who choose to be single. We should exhort single people to rise to the challenge to enjoy their singleness and make the most of its opportunities, but this must be in the context of a helpful and supportive body, not a disinterested, suspicious or patronising one. Let single Christians be recognised as the true equals of those who are married.

Widows in the Church

Of all the subgroups of single people, the ones given most attention in Scripture are widows. Widows were far more common than widowers then and still are. In about three out of four cases it is the husband who dies first. This is probably the main reason widowers are not specifically addressed. A widower, if younger, would still have been able to provide for himself economically, and so the same practical problems would be less likely to arise.

Provision for widows seems to have been made from the very foundation of the church (Acts 4:34–5). However, it quickly emerged that one group, the Aramaic speakers, were being better treated than those who spoke Greek. Straightaway, the church acted to put this right by appointing seven men to oversee the daily distribution of food (Acts 6:1–7).

Widows are free to remarry if they want to. They are not bound to their dead husband (1 Cor. 7:39). Widows of Roman citizens were subject to an imperial order issued in AD 9 which required them to remarry within two years of their husband's death, if they were still of childbearing age. This was deemed to be under 50.

The strongest statement of the church's responsibility is in the letter of James. He contrasts acts of religious worship with: 'Religion that God our Father accepts as pure and faultless is this: to look after orphans and widows in their distress and to keep oneself from being polluted by the world' (Jas. 1:27). This strong commitment to the marginalised of whatever description must mark our Christianity.

As the church grew and became more established, more detailed guidelines became necessary. In his first pastoral letter to Timothy, Paul spelled these out (1 Tim. 5:3–16):

- Honour those widows in real need (vv. 3, 5). Honour implies a degree of material support, not just respect.
- If widows have children or grandchildren who can look after them, then it is their Christian responsibility to do so. It is right that the family repay something of the love and care that they have previously received (vv. 4, 16).
- Provide help for the widows so that they are not forced to resort to immoral living to survive (vv. 5–8).
- Younger widows should be encouraged to

remarry, have children and live productive lives, not sponge off others (vv. 11–15).

- Older widows capable of working for the church were enrolled on a special list. The conditions were that they must be over 60, have been monogamous (NIV 'faithful') be known for their good deeds, such as rearing children, hospitality, humble service, helping the needy and general good works (vv. 9–10). They were also to be women of prayer and dependence on God (v. 5). Those on the list may have operated as officers of the church. In return for their material provision they were expected to continue their lifetime's service.

Today, the state provides a basic pension to all elderly widows. There is a less acute need for the church to provide for its widows and widowers. Many of them have a lifetime of Christian service behind them, so that they meet the requirements of the first-century 'official' widows. They represent an important resource within our churches and must not be overlooked.

Marriage and Celibacy as a Demonstration of the Kingdom of God

It has been suggested that in addition to the specific teaching in the New Testament we have studied, there is a further dimension. Celibacy is a symbol of the new order of the Kingdom of God.

When God created humanity as part of the physical world, marriage was the perfect answer to Adam's need of relationships and sexuality. When the Father sent Jesus to institute the Kingdom of God, His new spiritual order, Christ was the perfect example of fulfilled singleness. He was at peace with His sexuality and enjoyed a right relationship with God and His fellow men. David Gillett says: 'As in Adam, the first man in creation, we discover the perfection of marriage, so in Christ, the second Adam and the first man of the Kingdom, we are confronted with the perfection of singleness.'[18]

It is not just marriage, but also singleness that gives important insights into the Kingdom. Marriage is used as a picture of the perfect union of Christ and the church (Eph. 5:32). Celibacy is a sign of giving up all for Christ; it is one way of seeking first the Kingdom of God, a way of being in the world but not of it. In heaven there is no marriage; we will each be joined to Christ instead. Celibacy today is a foretaste of our heavenly relationships. Marriage is a reminder of the best of the old order of creation; celibacy is a reminder of the new perfect order to come. As the physical union of marriage is a picture of the blessings of the Kingdom, so responding to the call of celibacy is a picture of the cost of the Kingdom. In the Kingdom celibacy and marriage live side by side, a paradox. Neither is superior, they are options for the individual, and together they give a fuller model of the Kingdom of God, than either on its own. Max Thurian states:

Celibacy is one of the signs that remind us of the absolute demands of Christ, of His liberating return, of the establishing of the Kingdom of heaven and of the need to be watchful, to renounce the world, the flesh and covetous desires, and to welcome joyfully in our hearts the sacrifice of our passions in pure love for Jesus.[19]

He continues:

> To remain celibate for the Kingdom of heaven's sake is not to be less human, but to know life; in giving up one form of human existence the Christian finds fullness of life. Christ was no less human because He had no other love than that of His brothers and no other bride than the church.[20]

In response:

> Christians, both men and women, give up marriage, contrary to the order of creation which was faithfully observed in ancient Israel. They do this, not in order to choose a morally better way, but because, in the new order at the end of time in which we live, God places in His church the signs of the Kingdom of heaven, of which celibacy is one.[21]

The spirit has replaced the flesh as the most important dimension. Under the old order the priority was natural children, to continue the growth of God's people Israel. Under the new covenant the priority is spiritual children, to see people born again into the Kingdom of God. For the former to happen marriage was essential; for the latter, marriage is optional. The new priority has removed marriage from its place in Jewish society where it was a command—all must obey—to a matter of choice for each person.

Thurian and others believe in a lifelong call to celibacy as a parallel to marriage. He believes it requires an equal calling and commitment to that of marriage. He does not believe all single people have this calling. He suggests four signs of possessing the gift of celibacy:

- An inner witness of the Holy Spirit. An assurance of faith shown by joy and peace at the prospect of lifelong celibacy. It is often linked to a calling to a particular role which requires singleness, such as a form of Christian ministry.
- The person's particular circumstances.
- A clear decision, an act of faith in response to a call. Faith is necessary because one can never be sure by reasoning at the point of commitment what will transpire.
- The role of the church in confirming a call so that it does not depend on the subjective perspective of the individual alone.[22]

His view is refreshingly different. It is a necessary corrective to a 'marriage or nothing' minded church. One need not agree with his views in detail to recognise the missing dimension he highlights. A few Protestant communities exist in the Anglican, Reformed and charismatic circles where Christian celibates have made vows to serve the Lord in this way. Protestant missionaries, especially women, have often made less formal, but no less real, commitments to singleness. Is it not time for celibacy again to be taught as a mainline option for evangelical Christians?

A Little Bit of History

Recently I was interviewed on a local radio station after writing an article which said that single people were discriminated against in evangelical churches, because they were underrepresented in leadership. The interviewer, a practising Roman Catholic, asked me, 'How is it that single people are denied leadership in Protestant churches? In my church you cannot get anywhere unless you are single!'

To understand this we must briefly trace how the concept of celibacy developed in the early church. The ascetic tendencies we observed in the Corinthian church became a widespread problem. The prime influence was Greek philosophy. The Stoics and the Platonists both saw the body and its desires as a hindrance to the pursuit of truth. Elitist groups believed celibacy was a route to greater holiness.

This thinking invaded the church. Mainstream leaders such as Justin Martyr, Clement and Origen believed that sex within marriage was only for procreation. They positively advocated celibacy, even within marriage. Tertullian taught three species of virginity: that from birth, of happiness and innocence; that from second birth, the virginity of virtue (either marriage precluding sexual intercourse or preserving widowhood from choice); and a third grade, monogamy (but renouncing sexual intercourse), the virginity of moderation.[23]

In the second century parts of the Syrian church demanded marriage or a commitment to celibacy before baptism. The early heretic, Marcion, made celibacy a condition of church membership.

In the third century Jerome argued that marriage was inferior to celibacy. About an opponent he wrote, 'He puts marriage on a level with virginity, while I make it inferior; he declares that there is little or no difference between the two states; I claim there is a great deal.'[24]

Gradually, virginity became extolled more and more. Cyprian (d. 258) described virgins as, 'the wholesome and uncorrupted portion of God's flock, the joy of the master'.[25]

A Christian view of virginity as the essence of all virtues emerged. The church at this time began to develop a view of Mary 'Mother of God' as a perpetual virgin, out of a misplaced desire to protect her honour.

Ambrose (339–397) believed marriage disqualified a man from ordination, as marital sexual intercourse defiled the ministerial office. He taught that 'individual virgins represented, to perfection, the church, the virgin Bride of Christ'.[26]

The church has slowly accepted an unbiblical and unnatural asceticism which has lasted until modern times.

What was seen as good for everyone became required of the clergy. Initially, married clergy were acceptable as long as they were married before ordination. A single man, once ordained, must remain celibate. By the Council of Chalcedon in AD 451 only junior clergy, such as readers and singers, could be married. In AD 691, at the Council of Constantinople, the Eastern church confirmed its policy, which holds till the present day, that priests may be married before ordination, but bishops must either be celibate or separate from their wives.

In the Western church the general practice of clerical celibacy was inconsistently followed until the eleventh century, after which it was regularised.

The Reformers of the sixteenth century rejected compulsory celibacy on principle. Luther and Calvin were bachelors who eventually married. Luther was 42, and Calvin 30. Clerical celibacy had been widely abused. Scandals abounded as some priests gave in to sexual temptation amongst many other failings. Luther saw enforced celibacy as a cause of much immorality. Reacting, he wrote that those who had the gift of celibacy were 'rare, not one in a thousand'. He abolished the division between clergy and laity and with it the demand for celibacy.

Calvin believed in the practical superiority of celibacy but only as entered into voluntarily. At any time a man was free to marry. He taught that marriage and celibacy were morally equal.

Married clergy soon became normal in Protestant churches of all kinds. In the Thirty-nine Articles of the Church of England, Article Thirty-two is 'Of the marriage of priests'.

The Roman Catholic church reacted angrily to the Protestant position. The Council of Trent (1545–63) declared, 'If anyone says that the married state is to be preferred to the state of virginity or celibacy, and that it is not a better and more blessed thing to abide in virginity or celibacy than to be bound by marriage, let him be anathema'.[27]

The Catholic church regards clerical celibacy as a matter of ecclesiastical rather than divine law, allowing it to make exceptions, as for married priests joining the church from other denominations. Its position has remained unchanged since the Reformation.

Most Protestant churches have, meanwhile, stopped emphasising the positive view of celibacy for either its ministers, or for its members as a whole.

As G. D. Fee comments: 'Roman Catholicism has insisted on celibacy for its clergy, even though not all are gifted to be so; on the other hand, many Protestant groups will not ordain the single because marriage is the norm, and the singles are not quite trusted.'[28]

The calling to celibacy has withered on the vine of neglect. It is time to change.

Conclusion

Of the four great characters of New Testament history it is remarkable that three were single people. John the Baptist, Jesus and Paul were single; only Peter was married. This statement cannot be proved beyond doubt as Scripture gives only limited biographical information. It is the most likely understanding of the evidence we have. John, the ragged prophet of the wilderness, Jesus, the humble friend of sinners, and Paul, the pioneering intellectual and evangelist, were three men who put serving God before the privileges and demands of marriage. Peter, too, put the cause of Christ first. His family must have suffered accordingly. We do not know how he balanced his responsibilities towards his loved ones with those of his calling as an apostle. Peter probably said a hearty 'Amen' to Paul's comments about the divided interests, and the need for married men to live as if single because of the times they lived in (1 Cor. 7:29–32). He illustrates, by a kind of reverse example, some of the advantages of singleness Paul details.

Scripture, both by direct teaching and illustration from its characters, demonstrates a positive view of celibacy alongside marriage. There is an urgent need, at the close of the twentieth century, to rediscover a biblical balance. People are constantly being hurt because of an imbalance in our teaching, pastoral care and leadership structures. It is a sad fact that today, many evangelical churches would not permit John the Baptist, Paul or Jesus Himself even to lead a house group, because they are not married (they would probably ban Peter too, as he spends too little time with his family!). Paul claims that if one member suffers, the whole body suffers (1 Cor. 12:26). The whole church is much the poorer because of its failure properly to honour its single section. Married people, please don't be threatened by teaching on singleness. It is for your good too.

---

[1] The best recent theology of singleness is in a book on divorce. See Cornes, A., *Divorce and Remarriage* (London: Hodder & Stoughton, 1993), Ch. 3 and 7. Also useful though more brief is the Grove booklet, Gillett, D., Long, A. and Fowke, R., *A Place in the Family* (Nottingham: 1981), Ch.1.

[2] Ber. Rab. 17:5. Quoted in Cornes, op. cit., p. 54.

[3] Yebamoth 6.6. Quoted in Barclay, W., *A Plain Man's Guide to Ethics* (London: Fount, 1973), p. 100f.

[4] Yebamoth 62 b.

[5] Yebamoth 63b. Other sources suggest that ben Azzai was married but lived apart from his wife. See Goergen, D., *The Sexual Celibate* (London: SPCK , 1976), p. 6.

[6] Pesahim 113a.

[7]Pliny, *Natural History* 5.15.73. Quoted in Cornes, op. cit., p. 89. Pliny's statement may refer to only one community of the Essenes at Engedi as there is evidence that other Essenes were married.

[8]See France, R.T., *Matthew* T.N.T.C. (Leicester: IVP, 1985), p. 283.

[9]In contrast to Joanna whose husband, Chuza, is mentioned in the same short list, Susanna is listed alone. She obviously was able to use her wealth at will to support Jesus. It is possible that she was a wealthy widow, but we cannot know for sure.

[10]For a much fuller treatment of Jesus' teaching on divorce see Cornes, op. cit. or Heth, W.A. and Wenham, G.J., *Jesus and Divorce* (Nashville, Tenn.: Nelson, 1985).

[11]See Cornes, op. cit., p. 91f. and Tidball, D., unpublished London Bible College Pastoral Care lecture notes made available to the author.

[12]See Kruse, C., *The Second Epistle of Paul to the Corinthians*, T.N.T.C. (Leicester: IVP, 1987), p. 15f.

[13]Quoted in Morris, L., *The First Epistle of Paul to the Corinthians*, T.N.T.C. (Leicester: IVP, 1958), p. 17.

[14]Quoted in Chaffin, K. L., *The Communicators Commentary: 1,2 Corinthians* (Waco, Tex.: Word, 1985), p. 89.

[15]Thurian, M., *Marriage and Celibacy* (London: SCM, 1959), p. 67. Without endorsing all its views, in the opinion of the present author this is the best treatment of the subject available although it is long out of print.

[16]See Barrett, C. K., *The First Epistle to the Corinthians* (London: A & C Black, 1971), p. 161.

[17]See Bruce, F. F., *Paul: Apostle of the Free Spirit* (Exeter: Paternoster, 1977), p. 269f.

[18]Gillett, Long and Fowke, op. cit., p. 9.

[19]Thurian, op. cit., p. 50.

[20]ibid. p. 51.

[21]ibid. p. 52.

[22]ibid. p. 86f.

[23]Tertullian, *Exhortation to Chastity*, i, v. Quoted in White, R. E. O., *The Changing Continuity of Christian Ethics, Vol.2.* (Exeter: Paternoster, 1981), p. 45.

[24]Letter 48 to Pammachius, 2. Quoted in Keeling, M., *The Foundations of Christian Ethics* (Edinburgh: T. T. Clark, 1990), p. 90.

[25]White, op. cit. p. 46.

[26]ibid. p. 47.

[27]Council of Trent session 24, Canon 10, *Enchiridion Symbolorum*.

[28]Fee, G. D., *The First Epistle to the Corinthians* N.I.C. (Grand Rapids, Mich.: Eerdmans, 1987).

5

First Principles: A Philosophy of Singles Ministry

John Littlewood

Each fatherless family at some point begins to dream again and make plans for the future, but fears often stay with them, at times drowning out the hopes. Such families need encouragement every step of the way. They need friends they can love and trust to reassure them they are on the right track.

Katie Wiebe

There are as many reasons for being single as there are for being married. In other words we cannot pigeon-hole 'singles'. People are single for both positive and negative reasons, as are married people. It follows therefore that we have to recognise that there is not and cannot be a blueprint.

It is certain that human beings need social contact, and more than that, we need relationships that fulfil our need to be loved and to feel wanted. A good summary of what Jesus brings to us through the gospel is that 'we belong'. To be converted to Christ means that we are incorporated into His Body and we belong.

It follows that any philosophy of ministry for single people must begin by recognising that single people need special care on the part of the church. Singles were not a problem to St Paul; not only did he recognise their true conversion meant incorporation into the Body of Christ, but he commended widows and other potential outsiders to the fellowship of the church. We need to respond to the same challenge.

Society has in the past assumed that marriage is for everyone, although perhaps less so today. Also, in the past people stayed within family units, whilst today we all seek independence sooner and it is normal for single people to live away from home, and therefore in a more isolated position. We need to realise, however, that this does not naturally mean that we set up special groups. To set up special groups will mean that we isolate that group; we would need very special reasons for doing that.

In society today we recognise that a major disease is fragmentation and loneliness. We see people everywhere who are isolated and alone, perhaps within a crowd of people, yet feeling that they belong nowhere. In fact we all know it to be true that you can feel most alone when you are in a crowd, yet not feeling that you belong. At a party if you do not know many people, you can feel particularly alone, even when you have some good security within yourself.

In society today we have never had such a proliferation of clubs and groups for this or that interest, sport or professional group. That can be good, but a major intention of the church is that it will bring people together. At the Communion, as we kneel, we have the millionaire business executive next to the person on social security, we have the teenager next to the OAP who is next to the single mum, who in turn is next to the ex-convict, who is next to the policeman. This is as it should be, and reflects what conversion means. In the life of the church we should do all that we can to build up this incorporation of people into the Body of Christ. Anything we do therefore 'for singles' should begin from that vital principle.

Age and Background

It is also important, in any overall view of ministry to single people, for us to remember that age matters a great deal in the way that single people view themselves, as does how they have come to be single. The person who has never been married has quite different attitudes and feelings to the widowed person, or to the divorcee.

Single people who are in their twenties perhaps do not even consider themselves as 'single'; it is simply where they are at. They are busy with life and need to be encouraged to enjoy this time, to be allowed to grow and interact within the whole life of the church and to make relationships within its good environment.

Single people who are in their thirties have a different attitude to being single; there are certain facts that might mean it is all right or that it is beginning to be scary! It might well be true that life is so busy that there is little room for good relationships. Relationships might get in the way of career, etc. Again it is vital that within the life of the church they can feel accepted, loved and secure, encouraged to live a balanced life with a rhythm that allows for relationships.

Single people in their forties have yet another agenda; they have a settled life, probably by now very good, with friends and a home and a way of life that means it would be difficult to allow others to interfere with it! This I believe is a fairly new state: it is possible today for single people to be fulfilled in their singleness and to be independent in a way that was very difficult until recently, especially for women.

We could then speak about the fifties, sixties, seventies, eighties and following, all of which bring new opportunities and challenges. Within the church we need to take seriously the idea that each age has its 'specialness' and its 'ordinariness' within the life of the whole, and we have to see that each age and each individual is *included*, valued and is being encouraged to *bring to birth* that next stage of life that God has called them to enjoy.

However, and here we need great sensitivity, we have to face the fact that *all people* (both single and married) are damaged in how we are able to relate and live. This happens through the things we encounter and the way we relate to each other; we are damaged. This is to do with our fallen state of sin. We have all been hurt, and we all have defence mechanisms.

Therefore we know that amongst those who are single there will be some who have never felt loved in childhood, or have been hurt in some way, and this has meant that they feel less secure in making relationships. They long to 'belong' but they almost always put themselves 'at arm's length', perhaps by an unspoken reserve or by the reverse, a brashness or, very commonly, by being the joky person, the one who is always good for a laugh. But this external flippancy is in fact covering deep insecurity, and once a person has become the butt of others' jokes (the one who is spoken of as, 'Oh Liz, she is such fun, always a laugh, she never seems to mind her leg being pulled'), he or she is in fact being wounded.

Sadly, that front begun some time before as a mechanism for being included, is now the very mechanism for keeping that person *out*.

Some single people are single because they find it hard to make deep relationships. The church should be a place where they find the acceptance and love that heals and transforms.

The widowed need to have time to mourn, and yet to feel included in mixed company. The divorced are again a very special case, each one different, but it is vital that they are *within—'in fellowship'*.

It is only after noting all these points that we can begin to answer the question of how we offer an integrated, fulfilling ministry within the church to single people.

The Role of Special Groups

Do we have special groups at all? We might, but we would be wise to proceed with caution. We need to encourage the fellowship to be an embracing (a good word for singles!), all-including fellowship, that through its whole programme, and perhaps specially through the home/house groups, offers hospitality which is seen to be an important part of the life of the group. Hospitality is close to the heart of God.

Our God is Himself hospitable, offering Himself to us and inviting us to find in Him friendship and sustenance. Again, the Holy Communion spells out that factor of God's love. He makes Himself available to us around a table—He invites us to feed from Him and to find in Him our wholeness. We need to use that as our pattern for ministry.

Hospitality is, I believe, the key to the life of the church and sadly it is a lost feature in many, if not most of today's churches.

I believe that special groups have value for a limited period in our life, when we face some special need.

If a church has a lot of late teens and twenties, it might well have a group for them, a group that includes Bible study, helping them to have reasons for being where God is calling them to be and for being a holy people; but that group should also have a lot of fun, its chief aim being that during that important stage of life they are learning how to make good relationships and interrelationships within the family of God.

Older people need a group where they can meet to explore how it feels to be older and to be encouraged to feel good. I can see that old age today is exciting, because those who are retired today probably have more money/income and more energy than any group of pensioners before them. However, there is still fear of failing health and of becoming 'a burden', and we need within the church to have a philosophy that allows each and every age and period of life to have its proper value and to be able to reach forward. Jesus always wants to say to us 'Follow me' and when we ask Him where we are going, He always says 'Come and see'; in other words we are invited into adventure and we must go without any set agenda; life is for living, for reaching forward, for having our eyes fixed on Jesus, who is our perfecter. It is His work to do that in us, but our part is to be ready to go with Him.

The church needs an agenda that allows for this to

happen; it needs a philosophy that engenders this freedom of being.

Any special groups or interest groups should therefore be integrated into the whole life of the church. They need to cater for some special need and they should be 'short-term', helping the individual members either to achieve a specific aim or to move through some period of their life.

In my church we have an art group. Although the time it meets (on a weekday morning) means that some people are restricted from joining, it does allow a small group to gather together for a specific purpose and to enjoy one another. A women's fellowship, meeting in the afternoon, means that it is mainly older ladies, who enjoy being out at the right time for them and whose main aim is to have fellowship. This group is perhaps the most common in churches, and it can get stuck and become stagnant: older people often want to stick with what they know! A group for older people (most often that would mean widowed/single older people) needs to be a group well-led, a group that is inviting those at a senior age to give birth to things that they have always wanted to do, write something, research something, travel, visit, be a missionary or whatever.

I can see that a church needs to engender an atmosphere where people would know they could talk about anything that was of concern for them, either with one person, or with a small group, and then be encouraged to go and live that out. That would be for me a major philosophy of ministry.

Another group we had in a church I was previously involved with was one that met by public announcement about twice a year. That announcement invited all single people to a supper; it was then spelt out that the group would continue in an informal way: a small area of a notice board would be theirs and if anyone wanted to go to any meeting or social activity, rally or teaching day, concert, film, theatre, day trip, etc., they could put a notice up inviting others to join them. Others could then sign up and together a few would enjoy that event without any hassle of who was inviting who, and no one need feel left out. The group needed the six-month kick start for two reasons: people joining the church in between would not know of the system, and in reality it was true that once it got going, it was easy for a group to stop using the notice board and just invite one another directly, so missing out those who perhaps most needed that easy way of joining in. A real spin-off to that group was that married couples could join in; say a wife wanted to see a film, her husband could stay at home with the children, she could have a pleasant evening out with friends and all benefited.

I am keen to be heard to say that we need to integrate adult people into a living/loving/wholesome fellowship that is the Body of Christ. Groups for this or that category of people should be started only after great thought and prayer. They should not become parachurch groups, nor the reason why people are there. They should be assisting the true membership of the Body of Christ to develop and become what Christ is calling them into.

The philosophy of a church towards single people needs to be that they are of equal value to anyone else, they are whole in themselves and not just waiting to be fulfilled by marriage. For this time in their life they are single and in that singleness they are whole within the love of God for them. They might be damaged, they might not, they might need pastoral care, they might not, but this will apply to the marrieds in the same proportions. They could well be wealthy and making a major contribution to the church; they will probably take more than their fair share of the tasks within the church. They will make up a sizeable proportion of the church and they need to be recognised as part of the whole, and valued, as God values them, for themselves.

6

Pressure Points

Dave Pope

To live a barren sister all your life,
Chanting faint hymns to the cold fruitless moon.
Thrice blessed they that master so their blood,
To undergo such maiden pilgrimage;
But earthlier happy is the rose distill'd,
Than that which withering on the virgin thorn
Grows, lives, and dies, in single blessedness.

William Shakespeare,
A Midsummer Night's Dream

Yes, there's that word again, always cropping up in conversation, particularly when discussing health, wealth or generally coping with the stresses and strains of everyday life—pressure!

'How's life treating you?'

'Well, there's plenty of pressure, but we keep pressing on!'

'How are you doing?'

'OK. The last few months have been pressurised, but hopefully I'm making some progress.'

Everyone knows what it feels like to be under pressure; it is the levelling experience whether one is rich or poor, unemployed or working a 60-hour week, young or old, single or otherwise. But the key is knowing how to handle pressure—not trying to get rid of it! The latter creates more than it disperses.

Maybe this is fundamental to an understanding of what this chapter is all about. Singles can often be simplistic and, dare I say it, naïve, in their appreciation of what constitutes fulfilment and happiness. Striving to reduce pressure, perhaps created by loneliness, depression and low self-image, rarely achieves contentment and peace of mind, and usually creates the opposite. However, taking steps to identify the weak areas in one's life, and recognising vulnerability, is a major step forward in learning to handle the pressures often associated with singleness in a responsible and mature manner. Of course, that's more easily said than done. Although we often recognise the sources of disquiet, hurt and life style turbulence, admitting that we're not coping too well, accepting input, help and advice is a whole different ball game. There are none as independent as the single-minded who have resolved to fight their battles in a solo capacity!

The church has an important role to play in this respect, although I am anxious to preface my writing with a perspective that I feel has been lost in recent years. Churches should be like battleships and troop carriers—functioning to serve the cause of Christ and committed to mobilising and activating God's people. Unfortunately, one could be forgiven for failing to notice this characteristic at the present time, when we seem to have a flotilla of floating clinics and hospitals, committed to caring for the wounded and more geared to counselling those on board than sailing into enemy waters to deploy resources and personnel. There also seem to be an awful lot of people absorbed in manning the bilge-pumps—keeping the water of the world out of the superstructure. My concern is that as we look at ways whereby the church can be more useful in addressing some of the issues relating to singles, we do not forget her primary purpose. Jesus gave us a commission to go and tell, Pentecost provided the power and anointing, and the lifeboat went down the slipway carrying disciples to reach out and save those in need. Any measure of help and input for the crew was always with the end view of achieving this goal, and not to increase the comfort zone for the saints! Recognising pressure points and suggesting ways whereby the church can be more effective is addressed here, not as an end in itself, but as a way of making sure that all of the crew achieve full potential for the Kingdom.

Family Life

'Next Sunday morning is our family service. Boys and girls, don't forget to invite your parents. We would love to see you all with your mums and dads here with us next week.'

Recent research in our nation has shown that the average family consists of mum, dad and 2.4 children. All very interesting, although perhaps not the best basis on which to forge ahead and devise strategies and life style predictions, particularly when the incidents of divorce and separation are escalating at a rapid pace, and when increasingly the 2.4 children are without one of their parents. The single parent phenomenon is by no means a rare occurrence any more, and the average congregation across the nation reflects that this is indeed a regular characteristic of the people in the pews. And let's not fall into thinking that this is always represented by the single mum. Increasingly there are single dads in our congregations who have the responsibility of rearing children.

But let's leave the parent–child model for a few moments. In a recent survey geared to discovering information about single people and the church, it was discovered that near enough 40 per cent of the people in the average congregation fell into the singles category— not just single parents, but the never-marrieds, those rendered single by the loss of a life partner, the divorced and the separated, and indeed those who have chosen to remain single for whatever reason.

At a recent breakfast meeting specifically organised for church leaders with an interest in the potential of single people in the church, one gentleman turned up and apologised for the fact that he had really only come because of the curiosity factor, as the singles issue was not relevant in his church. He listened carefully as attendees were encouraged to examine their church populations and identify those living a single life style, and to consider ways of providing help and encouragement. A rather surprised gentleman left the breakfast that morning but returned to see me three days later to admit that he was staggered to realise that 42 per cent of his congregation were single, and he had never considered them in a specific way when thinking of church family life.

No criticism intended here, but I suggest that this is true for many leaders, ministers and pastors across our nation. And don't misunderstand me—I'm not trying to champion the cause of greater recognition, etc., and develop a 'special case' mentality. Not at all. What I'm concerned to do is to encourage ostriches to look around, recognise what is happening to people today, address the pastoral issues that are raised, and recognise the positive factors to the glory of God! And this begins to make itself known when the illustrations and the sermon may feature single people, when family life is described more widely and accurately than the traditional concept, and when church families are also encouraged to embrace singles into their reckoning, particularly as they may well constitute at least a third of the membership roll.

I for one have always been nervous about promoting special activities for specific populations within the church, but when properly organised and well integrated into the ongoing life and witness of the fellowship, I recognise the usefulness. Hence the existence of the ladies' class—a real pain when it is no more than an excuse for digestives and knitting patterns, but a real blessing when it enriches the life of the church and addresses the needs of women, single or otherwise, who need help and encouragement for whatever reason. On the same basis, there is a place for singles to meet together, not as a matchmaking forum or a mechanism for airing grievances against all and sundry, but to receive encouragement, teaching and to develop enthusiasm for developing all the potential in the single lifestyle.

Unfortunately, singles themselves, because of the perceived stigma sometimes associated with being single, are often reluctant to support such a group meeting and therefore never benefit from such a facility. My mind focuses on a recent mission in the north of England, where I was asked to devise a strategy to reach the people of the church and the town, and as part of that initiative I suggested a meeting for single people. The initial reaction was sceptical—who are these single people? Will they turn up? What will we do if they come? We will never get more than a dozen at the most! On the actual evening in question, 78 people sat down to a buffet-style meal, enjoyed some music and a relevant talk on the potential of singles in the '90s, and the latest information is that the organisers have agreed to plan future events for singles as part of the ongoing church programme.

The Relationship Pressure

'No man is an island'—a popular quotation, and a truth that emphasises that we all need people. Barbra Streisand sang, 'People, people who need people, are the luckiest people in the world.' Unfortunately she was not quite accurate, because people who need people are often the most unhappiest folk, particularly when friendships are not forthcoming. God made us all differently, and we all have varying needs and capacities. Some of us are never happy unless we have folk around us 90 per cent of the time, whereas for others, the desire for space, and freedom to be oneself, is a high priority. Aloneness we all need at some time or another. Loneliness is a very different issue and a real problem for many people. So what should the church be doing in this area? In one sense everything, and in another nothing.

   In terms of facilitating an integration of single people more fully into the family life of the church, much can be done. Mention has already been made of singles meeting from time to time, and attention could be given to including contributions from singles in 'family' services. Singles often need to be stretched in their abilities too, and where traditionally a person has always been allocated a particular area of responsibility, perhaps a change in role is the kind of challenge needed to help them reach their potential.

I'm always amused by the baby-sitting syndrome, and of course as single people tend to be seen as folk with time on their hands, many find themselves looking after junior whilst parents are out. No real problem here, unless of course the privilege is abused, but what about inviting the baby-sitter round for Sunday lunch and investing the same amount of time in that person's life? Many singles arrive for worship alone and leave alone, only to fellowship with the microwave and the remnant of Saturday night's takeaway. And what about the practicalities of living a single life style? Are there people in the church who would be prepared to be the first port of call when the fuses blow or the pipes burst, or when there's been a break-in?

There are of course many other areas where the church can be involved to help, and where it can benefit from the potential of single people, but there is one area which should be left well alone. No prizes for guessing—pairing singles off! Hence one basic piece of advice: stop the matchmaking. Contrived Sunday lunches that bring two singles together in the hope that—nudge nudge, wink wink—the hormones might bubble, should be struck off the agenda. Similarly, quips about being left on the shelf and unclaimed treasures only serve to unearth an attitude that should have been permanently buried many years ago.

I recently attended a conference and was asked to speak at a singles seminar. I agreed of course, but my blood boiled when some chinless wonder advertised the meeting in the event bulletin as being 'For those left on the shelf'. My opening remarks at that seminar, I'm afraid, lacked grace and charm towards the person who wrote such mindless rubbish, and I took great lengths to emphasise that if I was perceived as being on the shelf, I had in fact put it there, arranged the brackets and personally driven in the screws. It was my choice for that particular time.

I recognise that I irritate some single people because I am very content in my singleness. I know it is God's will for me at the present time. For those who don't have that calling, or who feel rejected, isolated or angry with God because of their status, then I appreciate that my positive attitude does not always come as an encouragement. But equally it is not helped by over-enthusiastic marrieds who whisper promises of prayer in the ears of those who are deemed to be 'part missing' if they are not hitched, or by sharing pious platitudes indicating that 'the Lord understands'. The point is, we are all called to be obedient to Him, in order to discover His will and purpose. My faith is big enough to leave Him to make matrimonial arrangements in His time . . . He doesn't need the help of any fixers! And if it doesn't happen, I must trust Him for the alternatives.

Leisure Time

Sorry to mention it again, but we are all different. Personality, work capacity, sleep requirement, energy level and interests vary enormously, and it is a sad indictment that the church is often slow to recognise this fact. Nowhere is this more evident than worship, when an overenthusiastic extrovert worship leader insists that everyone must smile from ear to ear and wave hands in the air to enter into the spiritual excitement of the celebration. Similarly for singles to be pushed into a planned style of programmed leisure activity usually achieves the same rating on the aversion scale.

But in being overzealous in the area of spiritual integrity, the church has forgotten that God also made us with a social capacity, and He does not frown when we enjoy a visit to the theatre or the local leisure centre. He smiles on His children when they enjoy the beauty of His creation and He must surely smile when grown adults get wildly excited about 22 men kicking a bag of wind around on a patch of grass, with the expressed desire of getting that spherical object into the back of a suspended piece of netting! Maybe that's why pubs are so popular with Joe Public. He can relax, often eat good food, quench his thirst, meet people, play games and switch off from the routine of 9 till 5. Some pubs even have comfortable chairs arranged around open fires where you don't need a mortgage to eat wholesome food!

The implications of this are obvious. Singles do need to be encouraged to take time out to do something different. Planned trips for groups to the theatre or the bowling alley that don't exclude marrieds can be refreshing, and occasionally hiring the function room at the local pub for a special event can also be worthwhile. Many single people can be workaholics, particularly when work replaces what social activity never brings, and church leadership may need to take the initiative in encouraging leisure activities to happen. The church badminton or squash league, a Trivial Pursuits evening, a fork buffet supper for singles prepared by couples and a pot luck meal for marrieds prepared by singles can provide a missing dimension, particularly if the ideas are extended and a programme of social and recreation activity developed.

Friendships

Although any interaction between people suggests a relationship, I specifically want to talk about friendship here, to make an important distinction between what I said earlier and what I now want to express. We live in a sex orientated society, where people are led to believe that what is most important is being attractive, so that relationships are easily formed that lead to fulfilment and happiness. Hence the consumer society where everything from cars to ice-cream is promoted on the basis that purchase of the products makes you more accessible and interesting to other people. And although we may smile we are all, from time to time, hoodwinked by this ploy. And the sad legacy of this attitude is that the quality and integrity of good friendships has often been beached.

If two people are seen to be enjoying each other's company, then there must be something more in the wind. Two people eating together in a restaurant implies a little more, and sitting by the same person for more than three services could surely be the first sign of a blooming romance, particularly if the two people have to share the same copy of *Songs of Fellowship*!

For people of the same sex to have lasting friendships is equally fraught with danger, and because of the current trends in society, it's not long before tongues wag and questioning glances come across the crowded room. Of course, we have to be aware of the dangers of conveying wrong impressions and causing

144

unnecessary vibrations, as we are living in a world that is tainted and where relationships come and go like ashes in the wind, leaving hurt trails in their wake. But what has happened to the role of quality friendships, where for all the right reasons, people genuinely want to help others and enjoy each other's company without necessarily being subconsciously frog-marched to the altar by others? Has the platonic friendship disappeared for good?

Perhaps the church needs to minister in this area to restore the integrity and faith in friendship. Someone needs to teach people how to make friends and how to establish quality friendships using quality time. The 'instant' phenomenon should belong to the coffee jar— not to people.

Low Self-Image

By far the majority of single people have a low opinion of themselves, sometimes precipitated by the fact that they blame themselves for not being attractive enough to the opposite sex—hence their unmarried state. Or because their partner has walked out, they blame themselves for not being the model husband or wife, and if they have lost a life partner, then this feeling is compounded by the dread of having to face the world alone without the established security, comfort and support. Sometimes this can be successfully hidden, and someone who is perceived to be 'very independent' has probably developed a highly-tuned sense of self-reliance to help cope with their perception of themselves.

Awareness of this should help the local fellowship

to respond at the right level, but it is rare to find a pastoral team that can handle this area sensitively, yet firmly. A basic requirement for anyone involved in pastoring is to listen. I often say that God made us with twice as many ears as mouths, but this is easily forgotten when we get into our 'Messiah mode'! Single people need to have access to listening ears that hear, much the same as all sections of the population, but where self-image is low, it is particularly important. Integrating singles into prayer triplets or home groups, with opportunity for sharing corporately and in a one-to-one situation, should be encouraged.

There are dangers of course—the listening ear can sometimes be taken for granted or even abused, and striking the right level of involvement is not always easy. The gift of discernment is terribly important. Discerning when it is right to send someone on their way, discerning when a person really is in trouble, discerning when someone is genuinely heading for a nervous breakdown. This awareness does not come easy, but to the 'person-sensitive' member, it is a ministry opportunity that should not be neglected. To pray with someone, to put a hand on the shoulder, if coming from someone who genuinely understands, is invaluable.

But beware! Just as single people can be easy prey to those wanting more than friendship, the potential for things to go wrong, even in the best controlled counselling environment, is always there. There are now single parents in our country who have been rendered single having opened their home and their ears to someone in trouble. Without ground rules, relationships can develop which can threaten an established marriage, and before long, there is another digit on the singles statistic. The potential of emotional attachment, physical attraction and unhealthy dependence can be realised very quickly, and the basic rules of counselling should be adhered to very precisely. It is always wise to organise same-sex helpers, or where this is not possible, a partner alongside counsellor or counsellee, particularly if facilities are used where there are not many people around.

Spiritual Maturity

The greatest input in the ministry of the local church has to be in the area of encouraging its members to walk close to God. Singles, marrieds, children, senior citizens—there is no discrimination here. And my experience is that where singles are recognised by their presence and potential, and the worship and teaching incorporates their contribution and needs, then the outcome is healthy for ministers and laity alike. And where there is the challenge of mission and evangelism, then it can all get very exciting.

Has anyone in your fellowship thought about sponsoring one of your mature singles to visit a mission worker, administering encouragement? What about the opportunity for short-term service? It can often be the case that a single person has the capacity to use his or her skills for a period of time on the mission field, and with the current economic situation and subsequent unemployment, this can be a real investment. But the initiative needs to come from leadership out of the challenge of ministry, geared to the people in the pews.

It goes without saying, I hope, that singles should be given responsibility in all areas of church ministry and organisation, providing of course they are suitable and spiritually 'together'. Beware, however of over-using the people who are perceived to be more available, and avoid giving them too much responsibility. Printing the church magazine on the antiquated duplicator at 11 o'clock at night could be the straw that breaks the camel's back, particularly if that same person is responsible for nine other areas of activity.

Let's return for a few moments to that word 'pressure'. It is often associated with stress, although the two are generally confused. Pressure causes stress, and the latter is the body's reaction to pressure and stressors, manifesting itself in symptoms familiar to many of us—nervous headaches, appetite loss, high blood pressure, tense muscles, etc. Watch out for these signs, and be honest enough to recognise the source. For a pastor this is a very important area to appreciate, and should encourage him to look beyond the physical problem and identify the real issues. This then helps in the provision of an effective basis for input and ministry.

One of my favourite exponents of life style management is Dr Denis Burkit, a noted authority on the role of life style in human health, who has written extensively on this subject. In one of his writings, he describes a group of people who are playing games on top of a cliff. As a result of some of the energetic interaction, some of the folk fall over the cliff and are seriously injured. 'What is the best solution to this problem?' quips Burkit who goes on to suggest two possibilities—a clinic at the foot of the cliff to treat casualties as they hurtle to the bottom, or guard rails to prevent accidents happening. The correct solution is obvious.

But this has tremendous relevance and application to so many members of our congregations, and particularly to single people who, for whatever reason, have no continuous opportunity to diffuse the surplus mental, physical, emotional and nervous energy that can accrue in the rough and tumble of life. The church has a responsibility to put up some guard rails: maybe in terms of people who can listen; perhaps providing a programme of social activity that people can enjoy and use for relaxation; in ministry that reaches the souls of needy people, and not merely well-worn sermonettes that tickle the ear and miss the heart. And let's not forget the provision of challenge that raises the profile of members from mere pew fillers to actual life changers. Single people should not be the sole motivation for building this kind of ministry, but they would certainly be one of the first groups to benefit, and the church would be stronger for it.

"A SINGLE PARENT EH ? THAT'S GREAT. WE NEED HELP IN THE CRECHE TODAY AND WE HATE SPLITTING FAMILIES UP."

7

Relationships and Sexuality
Sheena Gillies

Lovely Pamela, who was found
One sure way to get around
Goes to bed beneath this stone
Early, sober, and alone.[1]
> Richard Usborne (*Epitaph on a Party Girl*)

There are times when I just love to be on my own. I don't have to talk, reply to anyone or ask before I change the TV channel; I can listen to Jazz FM all day if I want, and leave dirty dishes unwashed!

However, at other times I really hate it. No one to do things with, no one to moan to after a pretty awful day, no one to say 'Sit down, I'll make you a cup of coffee', no one to share that private little achievement with, no one to join on a sudden lasagne trip, no one to cajole you out of yourself—'Oh, if only there was someone . . . '

A lot of the time we can schedule out the things which would bring on the 'poor-me-I'm-alone' syndrome. But sometimes we just get tired of being strong, mature and sensible and give in to 'God, I'm fed up being on my own. How can I possibly feel content and fulfilled as a Christian when I keep being felled at frequent intervals by this overwhelming need to be "not alone"?'

As single people, we then have a tendency to go on to make the deduction that it's because we're not married that we feel like this. But ask one of your honest married friends if they ever feel alone. It seems that marriage does not actually make it disappear. It may change shape slightly but there are times when the feeling of aloneness still gnaws and someone who really understands is just beyond their grasp. Then they blame their partner.

But the problem is in us, not our single state or our marriage partner. We all have an inbuilt need for others, a need for a quality of relationship and closeness. (In this chapter I will be using the words 'relationship' and 'friendship' fairly interchangeably.)

As Originally Intended

This was also God's analysis of the situation when He first saw humankind in action—it was 'not good for [him] to be alone' (Gen. 2:18).

It is interesting to reflect on the fact that when we accept God's forgiveness He restores in us the ability to relate to Him. Linking that with Jesus' teaching in Mark's Gospel about the two most important commandments—'Love . . . God with all your heart and . . . soul' and 'Love your neighbour as yourself' (Mark 12:30–31)—we see that relating to God and relating to those around are integral pieces of a Christian's life. It is almost as if my restored relationship with God is proved by my relating to the folks around me. Assurance of my acceptance with God should work itself out in my relationships with others. It seems that all human relationships were intended to reflect something of God's character. This seems to have little to do with being married or single.

But . . .

We live in a fallen world where things do not work quite as they were intended. And relationships between human beings are just one of the many things that do not work quite as intended, whether married or single! Frankly, we are disabled and struggle to cope with relationships. This is a trait of all human beings. Neither spouses, seminars nor surgery can remove it!

What interferes with us being able to make good relationships? Jealousy, selfishness, self-preoccupation, fear of being seen for who I really am, lack of trust for starters. All these came after the fall and produced a twistedness in human nature.

But our inability to handle relationships wisely does not remove the need for them—we still need to understand and be understood. It remains a basic need of *all* human beings and to fulfil that need there seems to be an endless search for this elusive someone who is always just out of reach, or at least not in my circle of acquaintances! And the lack of relationship brings pain and loneliness. The battle against loneliness will probably never stop for the single person—it's our badge of 'human-ness'.

However, our expectations of finding that kind of satisfaction from a friendship will always lead to disappointment. We are all 'tarred with the same brush' so that no human being can really meet that need adequately. In fact, only God can do that. But we still look for the impossible in our human relationships and are continually disappointed. We place incredibly high demands and expectations on other people who float into our orbit.

In a world where friendship or relationship is pursued with an ulterior motive, it is very difficult to enjoy friendship for its own sake. Single Christians are subjected to pressure in this area, because sadly the church is often no different to the tennis club or the pub when it comes to the motives for getting to know people—'I saw you sitting beside *him* again!' or 'You were talking to *her* again after the service!' All from well-meaning people.

Many relationships are about what we can get out of them, rather than an end in themselves. If I feel that my friendship is being cultivated for an ulterior motive, I will probably not be too available.

We cannot make relationships with others a substitute for meeting our own feelings of loneliness, rejection or other anger at life's unfairness. That is not friendship. If we do, then when we get hurt by someone we had wanted to trust, we retreat and dare not attempt to interact with any more of these hurtful, fallen human beings! But this will only worsen the pain of loneliness. Singleness often gets the blame, but is that a correct assessment?

We all have a need to be accepted for who we are. Closeness, acceptance, loyalty and trust are all important factors in our own development as a person as well as our spiritual character. Is marriage the only context in which this is possible? The Bible does not give that impression at all. It has friendships and relationships which show support, trust and loyalty between non-married people. The obvious example is the friendship between David and Jonathan (1 Sam. 20:17); also Jesus and His small group of disciples, with His inner circle of even closer and more trusted friends with whom He could be open. These are clear illustrations of good interaction at a friendship level.

The Bible has quite a lot to say about friendship and trust. Proverbs 17:17: 'A friend loves at all times.' That's asking a lot of some of us! But the Bible is also very realistic about the quirks of human nature. We also need to be sensitive and have respect for other people's needs and privacy: Proverbs 25:17 warns about us making a pest of ourselves. Married people also need space for themselves. We need to review our intentions, motives and methods in developing and maintaining friendship and relationship.

Who actually knows you enough to ask you real questions about what you're doing, without you desperately defending yourself or just sulking? Who can give you an honest appraisal of what you're doing for your own good, to build you up and not leave you a trembling, defeated heap?

That seems to be part of the intention in God's plan for companionship and relationship (Gen. 2:18).

His and Hers

The crunch point is relationships between members of the opposite sex. We are made male and female to complement one another and in some amazing way, man and woman together express God's image (Gen. 1:27), so we need the company of the opposite sex in order to be fully ourselves.

But that's the theory! The actuality of living is rather complex with all of the pressures and expectations that we have to cope with. Social life for many Christian single people is as enjoyable as walking the gangplank!

Is it possible to have an open and trusting relationship with a Christian of the opposite sex without any strings attached? Is marriage always the goal in mind or can the friendship be an end in itself? I have put this question to quite a number of men and women. The replies come back as 'yes', 'no' and 'I don't know' in about equal numbers. I would suggest that there are inevitably pressures because of our biological make-up and reaction mechanisms as well as the pressure of other people's expectations. So we have to be realistic and impose some limits and safeguards. At some stage in a friendship between a man and a woman, it is very likely that feelings are aroused just because of relative closeness and natural tendencies. But I think that it is possible to have a good friendship once you have cleared the ground and been totally open and honest with each other. However, if you are single and hating it, the chances of your being able to see a man as anything other than a potential mate are probably quite slim!

To observe a man-eating woman in action is an awful sight. But the predatory male skulking around is equally awful for the observer, to say nothing of the prey!

Picture the church social event of the year—the Harvest Supper. There are those who are paralysed and sitting as tight as they can in their seats, terrified to speak to someone or even look in a particular direction for fear that they might be misunderstood. But then there are the ones offering around every plate of sausage rolls that they can lay their hands on in an effort to 'survey the field'. It has been likened to swimming in a pool of piranha fish. In fact I think I would opt for the piranhas!

If I find myself the target of unwelcome advances, I usually avoid that person even if it takes effort in maybe coming off a committee. Or I take a good male friend into my confidence and have him shadow me for a bit when the other is around. This can be quite effective. Conversely, I have been involved several times by some of my good male friends in this 'smoke-screen' capacity. It can even be fun and usually does the trick. In addition, the trust and friendship between you and your ally is actually strengthened and affirmed.

When we are thrown together with people in church, say to serve on a committee or maybe in the same house group, all kinds of dynamics and agendas can be going on in spite of what we do to avoid it—the fellow with the trousers that are too short who always offers you a lift home, the girl who keeps changing her seat to be near to a particular person, the married chap who tells you that you are so understanding, or the leader who considers that because you are single you must have lots of spare time to do all the administration for the group.

How, in those kinds of situations, can you possibly be relaxed and attempt to relate normally when you have to keep all your wits about you and take continual avoiding action? It's not an easy one!

How Can We Reclaim and Redeem Real Friendship in a Fallen World?

As redeemed individuals we have, in theory, the ability to understand relationship as originally intended by God. However, the thought of achieving it is rather like attempting the north face of the Eiger. How can we begin to clear our minds and behaviour patterns of all that has been fed in by a secular world whose motives and goals are in a different league altogether? Relationships in the world's intentions are mostly to meet my own needs—sexual satisfaction, useful contacts, alleviating loneliness or just in order to be seen with someone and be 'normal'.

As Christians the bottom line must always be that the relationship is honouring to God. Does this friendship enhance my spiritual life and does it bring credit to Christ's Kingdom? When I am affirmed by my friendship am I a better person for others to be around and more approachable to others? Good relationship should free us to be more ourselves. Because I am accepted by someone else, I can actually accept myself more, get on with life and leave some of the hang-ups behind.

Starting Point

We need to examine our behaviour and actions when it comes to other people. What draws us to people? What determines whether we pursue a friendship or just let it die quietly? An honest answer to this question may give us a clue as to how we view relationship and indicate our needs and attitudes to friendship and relationship.

Some Pointers

Real friendship is about sharing. There must be a mutuality, a two-way thing. If one person is doing all the supporting all the time there is something wrong with the balance of the friendship. In the biological world it would be called a parasitic relationship. One is being drained at the other's expense. This is not unusual in our sick and sad world. Many people need a lot of support. But maybe this is not the kind of person with whom you would spend the amount of time that you would with a friend. Choose your friends carefully. Pray for and cultivate one or two people who will be real friends. Prioritise ones with whom you can be really open, honest and trusting—two or three at any one time, the model that Jesus showed.

Be realistic about spending time with friends around other commitments and responsibilities. Friendship cannot be rushed; it develops over time but we do need to set time aside to invest in friends.

Relating to other people and organising things can be a little daunting at times if you are one of the many who are not super-confident social organisers. A great way to get around this is to do things on the spur of the moment—people have no great expectations and will enjoy impromptu coffee at your home. It's easy to provide coffee and a venue for other people to relate to one another. In larger cities, where there are not natural community meeting places, we have to make these happen; it's so important for people to interact with other people (not necessarily all single).

It helps when we know ourselves and so understand what kind of friends we need, both male and female. And we need to be able to communicate those needs to the friends, so that we all know where we are.

The balance of men and women in the average church makes some of this possible only in our dreams! Actually the statistics show that under 30, the balance of men and women in the church is about equal. It only gets out of kilter after that. But we do need to try to keep that balance somehow. I have been very fortunate in my working situations, where the balance has been weighted towards the male side. And no, I will not change places with you even for a day! But I do so value my male colleagues and their opinions even if they are chauvinistic at times—at least I have earned the right to tell them so. Sometimes they even listen! I know that I react quite differently in a mixed group, but then I should expect a difference because that's what God's ideal grouping is—male and female together.

In most churches there are married couples (one of whom must be male!) even if the single male population is thin on the ground. They can help keep that balanced perspective and give the male opinion. You have to be careful then that you spend as much time with the wife as you do with the husband, for the obvious reasons. But it is important—as well as enjoyable!—to have married couples in our circle of friends. This also helps to keep friendship in a broader context than that of potential marriage.

Beware of exclusiveness in friendship. Other

160

people should not feel like intruders when in the company of you and your friend. If they do, there is something wrong with the relationship. Jealousy, possessiveness, dependency and the like are all injurious to real friendship. They do not allow the freedom to be yourself that is the intention of a real friendship.

It is the 'Christ-factor' that will make the difference in relationships between Christians. That will determine and control our goals and our behaviour.

Are Single People Asexual?

The sex ingredient in relationships is a fascinating one. Sexuality is quite a difficult thing to define. What makes me feminine apart from anatomy? Does it make any difference in my approach to things? We are all so conditioned by our culture that we tend to reduce sexuality to the sex act between men and women. But that is to reduce my sexuality which is expressed in many more ways than just physically in bed. It is expressed in my opinions, my actions, my reactions, the way I look after my home, the way I express concern and care. But my female expression needs to be complemented by a male expression on the same things. Then we have the kind of complementarity that God intended when He made man and woman to display His image. So all of God's people, single and married, need each other, and sexuality goes beyond the physical.

No one can be male or female in the abstract. We are male and female as we encounter the opposite sex. It is only then that our sexuality is experienced and, as pictured in Genesis 2, we know what it means to be fully created in the image of God. Sexuality is the mystery of our need to reach out and interact with others, both physically and spiritually. But it is part of God's design that the strong physical drive is meshed with our ability to love and care. Sexuality also gives the strong desire to be loved and for physical intimacy. But God's design for intimate fellowship between man and woman is broader than the physical. We all need and desire spiritual and emotional intimacy. Sometimes this need may get confused with the sexual desire for physical expression. It is important to remember the difference, because this is not what is being fed to us by the world.

So sexuality is very much part of the single person's life, although the ultimate expression of that complementarity in intercourse is denied to the single Christian—that is reserved by God for the marriage relationship as an expression of total commitment and openness.

Relationships then, in a Christian context, become expressions of our experience of God's love and an affirmation that we are created in God's image, male and female. Sexuality is that which draws us towards loving relationships and then is expressed as a deep care and concern for others.

The traditional characteristics of femininity have taken quite a shift in recent times, along with the rules on the roles appropriate for women. It is quite difficult to know now what exactly demonstrates 'woman-liness' and what is cultural. Men so often label strength of character or assertiveness as non-feminine. But with women who have had to claw their way to the top to survive in a world that only recognises jungle tactics, some of those traits are occupational hazards and necessary for work. Very often, because men are threatened by what they call 'strong women', they give them a wide berth in a social context.

A great many Christian women feel that they have to resort to and reduce themselves to the world's expressions of sexuality in order to attract a husband, because that is all that they are hearing. The despair that exists among many single women could be lightened if we could grasp how to develop our female sexuality without waiting for a man to do it for us. So many women are made to think that they are defective because no one has yet chosen to marry them, so they will do almost anything to prove that they are valuable. But the fact of the matter is that unless we face up to reality and accept the fact that God does not guarantee a husband, we will go on living in 'never-never-land' and believing the myth that all we need to do is to believe God for a mate! But the amazing thing is that He does actually promise us fulfilment. This must mean, by deduction, that I can experience satisfaction and fulfilment in relationships without sexual intercourse.

We would not be true to our God-given design if we pretended that the desire for physical relationship is not extremely powerful at times. It can be triggered by all sorts of things, and we probably know our particular areas of vulnerability. It is a natural mechanism built in by the Master designer, but how we deal with it is the real issue. How do single people release the tension that builds up? We have to know ourselves, recognise what causes the tension and find ways of realistically reducing the tension. The cold bath is a bit extreme! But actually, redirecting your attention or focus (which the cold bath also probably does!) is a good way. It is often one thing in particular which prompts the thought and desire, so remove that one thing or remove yourself!

Pairs and Spares

Sadly, in our churches the great band of the unmarried are very often confirmed in their feelings of failure and dissatisfaction by being overlooked in appointments and tasks of responsibility. Marriage seems to be the unspoken rite of passage to maturity and to the ability to be stable and cope with responsibility. Or are married women more reliable or even safer just because they have someone they must answer to, whereas single women do not?

The suspicion and distance with which some single people, both men and women, are handled in church can be quite damaging or at least hurtful. Of course it has to be acknowledged that there are some people with whom we do have to be careful—in what we ask them to do or who we ask them to work with. Maybe in those cases, more careful oversight could be given.

Nor can it be said that single people cannot be involved in general pastoral care because they 'won't understand'. We all, single or married, have limitations on our ability to understand another's situation and empathise with them. Our marital status is not actually a very accurate measure of our ability to understand! We must be careful not to tar everyone with the same brush and squander such a pool of God-given gifts and resources.

164

He Knows Me Better Than I Know Myself!

Our maleness and femaleness are God-given gifts for our enrichment in all relationships. We need to affirm one another in our respective contributions rather than fear them. We need one another so that we can be fully ourselves.

The Apostle Paul knew so well how his response to the living God had changed his life, had given it purpose and meaning and had taken him through all sorts of situations. So he could say with certainty to those in Corinth asking about singleness and marriage (1 Cor. 7:24, 32) that, 'Whatever you are, don't worry about it!' He could say that not out of flippancy but because he knew that God desires our good and that wholeness is His goal for each of us, no matter whether we are single or otherwise.

---

[1] Quotation from Cohen, J. M. and M. J., *The Penguin Dictionary of Modern Quotations*, revised edition (Harmondsworth: Penguin Books, 1980).

"YES MRS PERKINS I QUITE UNDERSTAND YOU DIDN'T WANT TO DISTURB THE MARRIED STAFF AT 3.00 AM BUT I'M AFRAID THAT COUNSELLING FOR INSOMNIA ISN'T REALLY MY SCENE."

8

Getting It Right in the Local Church

Roger Welch

*When I was in my twenties and early thirties, I was
fully expecting to marry, but when the moment of
decision came I lacked assurance that this was God's
will, and so drew back. I began to ask myself at that
time whether God was calling me to be single. I have
never had a revelation from God. I have never taken
vows of celibacy. It's been the force of circumstances.*[1]

Revd John R. W. Stott,
Rector Emeritus, All Souls, Langham Place,
London

A humid afternoon in West Africa. I had been
invited, after several days of Bible ministry, to sit
in on a business session of a missionary group.
The main business was the selection of a new leader for
the group. Their existing leader and his wife had been in
their role for the best part of a decade; they needed, and
were looking forward to, a rest. There were several
good candidates for the leadership role, but the
discussion centred largely around one man who, it
seemed, had all the necessary gifts and abilities to be the
team leader, pastor, government relations officer and

model for new and younger missionaries just beginning their work.

There was but one significant and major problem—this man, an experienced missionary in his late thirties, was single. How could he possibly lead this group? He would neither know nor understand the needs, especially of the single women in the group and, more importantly, he could not, of course, be their pastor in an intimate sense. The missionaries, many of them with a quarter-century or more of experience, wrestled and grappled with the situation. It seemed to be the single women who had the most difficulty with appointing a single man to be the leader. In the end, after discussion and prayer, a vote was taken and the man was elected.

Would that have happened in a European church?

Consider the church you attend. What proportion of the congregation is made up of single people? That is, all categories of singles. By all categories, I mean the never-married, the separated and divorced, the widowed and those who are married—or in stable relationships—but whose spouses or partners are not involved in church life. There are probably not many people who are actually exercising a leadership function from any of those groups. Judging by all the statistics already quoted in this book, that is a sign that there is something wrong in the way the church ministers to, and receives the ministry of, single people.

How can we right this wrong? How can we grapple with this apparent injustice? How can we actually begin to make better use of the gifts and abilities that God has placed in the church in single people? It is extraordinary, isn't it, that through the last 200 years, we have looked to, and encouraged, single people to have extensive ministries in the overseas church in evangelism, church-planting, Bible translation and all the various supporting activities, but we have not used such people in leadership in the majority of Western churches.

Of course, in the Catholic tradition, there is the fact of the single, male priest and the single male and female religious orders. That we take as read; they are not under discussion here.

In this chapter I want first to look at some of the problems in promoting the leadership and ministry of single people in the church, and then make some suggestions about how a typical small or medium-sized church could approach the issue so as to improve its performance, record and perhaps the quality of its ministry.

Economies of Size

The majority of churches in Britain and Europe have less than 100 people in membership and attendance. Unfortunately most models of ministry come from churches that are very much larger and especially from churches that have significant numbers of young, single and married adults. The statistics show that, whether a church is small or large, it will have a significant proportion of single people in it, but the proportion of single people in different categories changes significantly as the size of the church grows. In particular, a smaller church will tend to have few young, adult, single people. The reasons are very simple:

1. **No young people.** It is one of the biggest frustrations for the leaders of small churches that the

larger churches seem to take all the young people. It is part of the very old syndrome that if you have, you can get; if you haven't, you can't get. Most small churches lose the majority of their young, single adults between the ages of 16 and 25 to university, marriage, work or simply through disillusionment and backsliding.

Only two things can really stop this rot. It needs either a revolution in ministry towards young, single people, or a revelation of the Spirit that actually brings young people into the church.

In my personal experience it was actually the second. Arriving in a new church, my wife and I were told that there had been a prophecy that the Lord was going to bring young people into the church. We looked at the congregation; the teenagers could be counted on one hand. We were sceptical about the prophecy, but reckoned that if we worked hard for five or six years and developed the right structure of ministry towards children and early teens, then maybe we would eventually have a thriving young people's work. It was after only a few weeks of ministry that we were visited one night by two or three young people representing a group who were looking for a church to call their spiritual home. One week later I was astonished to walk into the church for the evening service and find the front two rows filled with young teenagers. They were not there to be difficult, to criticise or in any way to disrupt; they were there to participate, to learn and to get involved. For a decade the church's ministry to young people, and therefore its ability to attract single people in their late teens and twenties, was revolutionised by that one act, which was a sovereign one by God and nothing to do with any structures or teaching programme that had been undertaken.

2. **The pull of numbers.** Family circumstances have brought Jenny home. She is a single Christian in her late twenties and, through work and college, has been away from home for some time. Now she has returned to live with her widowed mother. When she was a student she used to attend our church quite regularly, but I noticed that she had not been doing so since she returned home. I gently questioned her mother about it because I noticed Mum too had been missing from church a bit. She explained with pleasure, but also with sensitivity, that if Jenny was ever really to grow as a Christian and to enjoy friendship with Christians of both like age and like interests, she would not do so in our estate-based church. So both mother and daughter had been travelling into the middle of the city so that Jenny could get settled into a church with an outstanding international reputation in which there were hundreds of young single adults. Among those hundreds there was inevitably a group who shared Jenny's interests and outlook, and into which she had fitted in a way which was making this one of the most productive and blessed periods of her Christian life.

What church leader can possibly stand against that kind of spiritual move and blessing? Of course it would have been great to have Jenny among us. She could have been so 'useful'. She could have participated in the worship, perhaps taught in the Sunday school, used some particular gift she has to encourage some of our children. She could have got involved in a home group and mixed with others of her own age. But she would have found very few who shared her particular outlook and interests and certainly would have found the prospects of meeting a single Christian male to whom

171

she might be attracted pretty remote.

What do you make of that? Are you incensed by it? Or do you feel it is inevitable? Maybe you are one of those young adult singles who are faithfully persevering in a smaller church. Let me assure you that we need you, but we understand when you feel you need to go to fish in bigger lakes.

So really this needs to be two chapters: one on what the small and middle-sized church can do, having probably few people in the young adult singles group; then one on what the larger church is already doing, or should be doing, to develop the ministry and leadership of singles.

But that is to talk about only one category of single person—the young adult. Most writing and thought does tend to concentrate on that particular category. Accepting that, let us grab back all those who belong to those other categories of singles and say something about what already exists in most churches for most of them.

In most churches most single people are in some way attached to a group in which there are others like themselves.

They are found in such places as youth groups, twenties groups, women's Bible study groups, women's fellowships, men's fellowships and the like. Many find real support through groups like mums and toddlers where a significant number of mums may be single. In other words, structures already exist to develop the ministry and leadership of single people. But how often do you find that it is the stable, married ones who are actually appointed to lead even those kinds of groups?

Felt Needs

In all the discussions I have had with single people as a pastor, certain feelings and needs seem to surface which expose and reflect the ministry of this, and some other, churches. The greatest needs seem to be as follows:

1.   **Recognition.** In the eyes of many single people, the church does not recognise their existence. We talk a lot about reaching 'the whole family', which is taken to mean, by many singles—especially young adult singles—families where there are children. That means, of course, families where there are married people, divorced people or older people. We have family services which simply seem to reinforce the whole idea that church is for people who can produce a 'normal' type of family structure.

2.   **Appreciation.** Singleness is constantly spoken of as a kind of problem. It may be the 'problem' of adults in their thirties, forties or older who have never been married, and for whom a ministry and an outlet for relationships need to be fostered in the church. It may be the 'problem' of dealing with single parents or with the elderly living alone. Whichever way it is focused, it always seems to come out that singles are a 'problem'. As long as this attitude remains, single people will feel unappreciated by those who are not single; the ministry of singles will be marginalised and ministry to singles will be irrelevant.

3.   **Acceptance.** 'Accepted' also   means supported. Prevailing attitudes towards single people expressed in many churches leave them feeling both neglected and alone. The only way they can find acceptance is by serving well within the parameters that

a church establishes. The classic case is that the single lady, once she is over about the age of 23/24, is regularly used for baby-sitting services for her contemporaries who have children.

Many single people, like single parents, find that they actually need to get together in order to feel any kind of support. 'Nuclear' families tend especially to be rather insular and closed units; single people are very hesitant about intruding on their privacy. The result is loneliness and a sense of not really being accepted for the people they are. What then can, or should, be done by the church? Whatever happens it can only be effectively done by individual congregations (most of which, remember, are under the magic number 100 in size).

Our greatest need is for a change in leadership attitude towards single people.
Unless this happens, the rest of what follows is, at best, a set of good ideas which could only be partially implemented. The church has accepted, and developed, a theology which places the nuclear family in the position of being God's basic building block in society. This building block is sometimes added to by necessity and is extended to include other generations that are attached to the nuclear unit. However, the nuclear unit basically reigns supreme. The alternatives of community living have rarely been successful. They are perceived as being appropriate for only a small number of people, and most appropriate perhaps for a number of single young adults.

Changes in attitude need to begin therefore with leaders. They, above all, need to consider their theology of the family and personhood. If they have not got it right, then they cannot possibly lead the church into truth. I would recommend that leaders consider working through the EA Singularly Significant pack, as well as the earlier chapters of this book, to establish a theology of the family and of singleness.

Leadership teams are often exclusively male and married. To be realistic therefore, many might need to include, at some point in their discussions, those who are female and/or single. This study might just lead to conviction, and even conversion to a different attitude towards singleness in the church.

When attitudes are right a planned programme for educating others could be successful.
Once the leadership team has really got hold of the issue with vision, it should be passing it on through the various church groups. A possible programme might include:

1. **A sermon series.** It would need to be brief and cover the whole theology of the family, not just the issue of singleness. This would preferably include study notes, testimonies and other input from singles as well as married people.

2. **House group materials.** One of the best teaching methods, in churches where interaction is not common between pulpit and pew, is the follow-up of pulpit material in small group studies. In such groups, single people could bring their particular insights to the issues involved. It would be important for these groups to include homogeneous, same-interest groups within the church as well as perhaps the heterogeneous house groups that tend to dominate churches. So it would be good for the youth group, for women's Bible study groups, for single parent support groups, for all groups

175

possible actually to interact together with this material.

3. **A programme for the development of single leaders.** The existing imbalance in leadership teams is serious enough to suggest the need for 'positive discrimination' towards single people. That may seem too strong and unbiblical. We want called and equipped leaders. True. But that will surely include single people so, if we find a pattern of selection and equipping that excludes them, we need to take radical action to put it right.

4. **A plan for the review of our progress.** There needs to be a time-based review of our progress, perhaps done within a small team appointed from the leadership/membership of the church for that purpose. In most churches changes could be expected within a year of the completion of the whole-church teaching programme.

What about the church's ministry to singles?

If my single friends and my correspondents are typical, the last thing that most single people want is separate activities for singles. What they do want is to be integrated into the life of a local church, with their own personality and personhood accepted and respected. Teaching on 'the church family' and on the contribution of different people with their gifts in the church family, wo⁻ ld be a revolutionary way of tackling the singles 'issue' in most churches.

If the *ministry of single people* is appreciated and accepted in the church, then it is likely that *ministry to single people* will be effective. If a theology of the family, singleness and personhood is well worked out in a church and taught in both the pulpit and in small groups, then the change in attitudes brought about may well release many single people into ministries they have not hitherto had. There is, of course, no reason why any level of church leadership should exclude single people. However, there are certain areas where there seems to be a real mental block on the part of church leaders. None is greater than the predominance of married couples leading the small groups in churches. Why should it not be considered possible that a single person (or two single people), male or female, is as capable of leading a church house group as is a married couple? It is normally assumed that, where married couples lead, one of them has the leading role. No prizes for guessing which one!

The recognition and establishment of singles in positions of leadership, outside children's work and singles groups, would perhaps do more than anything else to raise the esteem and sense of acceptance and recognition of single people in most churches.
This would especially be the case if single people were to be found in what are recognised as teaching and pastoral roles, as well as in other areas of service such as evangelism and administration.

I recommend, therefore, a frank and open discussion with, or survey of, singles of all categories to discover what needs they have that are not being met in the church. Some needs may turn out to be legitimate and others may be needs that the church does not feel able, or called, to meet. Any survey should exclude suggestions or promises of action which are not really intended.

Conclusion

Most single people do not feel called to emulate the Apostle Paul, Dame Julian of Norwich or Amy Carmichael. In other words, they do not see themselves as having world-changing, or nation-changing, ministries. They do not expect to be overseas missionaries, nor even pastors or teachers; the majority of married people are none of those either.

What singles do expect is to be recognised, accepted and loved in their local church. They expect that the gifts God has given them will be recognised and used for the blessing of that church and its mission. They expect to hear Bible teaching, especially application of Bible teaching, which speaks to them in their particular state as single people. They do not want to have many activities organised for them which reinforce the fact of their singleness. They expect to be regarded as members of a church family and therefore treated with the same dignity and respect as every married member of that church family.

In the last generation the church has responded with energy and commitment to the needs of the married in our society. The growing incidence of divorce, marital breakdown and family problems has brought an explosion of ministries to the family and married couples. How about publishers putting a brake on that constant flow of books on marriage, recognising that we have enough now to be able to get it right if we are ever going to?

Instead, how about the '90s being a time when books flow on the subject of the church family; of integrating each person into an every-member-ministry in the church; of recognising the needs of children and young people, of the divorced and widowed, of the single and disadvantaged? How about a decade in which the church really does begin to be seen as a transforming agency for the whole family and therefore for society?

---

[1]Interview for *Christian Bookseller*.

9

Models of Ministry:
A Case Study of Basingstoke
Community Church

Dave Richards

I think I can honestly say that most of the time through those bachelor years the sense of God's companionship was real and satisfying. But it would be failing in honesty not to admit that awful moments of loneliness would suddenly descend on one, perhaps at weekends or else right after an exhausting and demanding mission. At such times I would either fight a mighty spiritual battle or else drift back in confusion or disobedience into former relationships which were not working out.[1]

Revd Michael Cassidy,
Founder of Africa Enterprise

What lessons can be learned from a church that takes the ministry of single people seriously? Basingstoke Community Church is a well-known New Church with 200 single people. We have an active programme of pastoral care, social action in the community, local evangelism and world mission. Single adults play an important part in our activities. We have learned a lot both from our successes and our failures which we hope will benefit others.

The church is divided into eleven congregations, meeting weekly in their geographical areas, with a monthly celebration for the whole church. This gives multiple opportunities for ministry, as every congregation has its own teams for leadership, worship, teaching, youth, where applicable, and children's work. Five of the congregations also have secular youth works attached. We also have a very active Pregnancy Crisis Centre operating from our main pastoral base, all of which gives room for many people to function.

The Vision

The issue of ministry is not 'married or single' but availability and calling. One of the most exciting things to observe in the Body of Christ is a man or woman fulfilling the call and destiny of God in their life. They are people who are not pining, nor wishing, nor even dreaming but acting upon God's directive to the work to which they have been called. One of my favourite Scriptures is 1 Timothy 1:18 where Paul, a father in the Lord, says to his spiritual son Timothy, 'This charge I commit to you Timothy, my son, in accordance to the prophetic utterances which pointed to you, that inspired by them you may wage the good warfare, holding faith and a good conscience (RSV).'

When we have clear prophetic direction over our lives, and spiritual fathers to guide and encourage us, then we can firmly grasp hold of our callings in a secure atmosphere to fulfil God's will in our lives. It is our desire to create such an atmosphere in our church. Our fellowship has a call to the nations like that given to the church in Antioch (Acts 13:1–3). At present we are involved in over twenty countries, with many people having been sent out as workers.

There has been a real desire in our hearts to discover and release gifts and ministries within our people. Character and content always precede charisma in our recognition and development of ministry, and faithfulness in the little things (Luke 16:10–12) is always a criterion upon which we base our judgements in releasing people to their true role in God's calling. Accountability and clear communication are also the order of the day because as we release trust, so we expect responsibility. What a joy it has been then to see so many single people fulfilling their God-ordained roles.

International Mission

Mission is a vital priority in our work and Uganda is a major field for Salt and Light Ministries, of which we are a part. Our first worker there was Annie, a single lady, who had been a full-time biology teacher in our Christian school. She was sent out in 1985, and since then has developed five schools with another two in the pipeline. Annie is a model of faith and courage to our church. She has survived armed robbery and many dangerous encounters to fulfil a deep longing in her heart to serve the people and churches of Uganda. Annie has hosted many teams of young people from churches in the West to further their development in God. She has been followed by another single girl, Pat, specialising in special needs education, which we hope will lead to major new openings in the nation. Recently the President's wife opened one of the new schools and the two women began a relationship. God can open large doors!

Debbie first visited Zimbabwe with a team I led in 1987. She fell in love with Africa, left nursing and now at the age of 30 runs an orphanage for 40 street boys in Beira, Mozambique. She is learning Portuguese as she preaches and cares. Debbie is a model of courage and care for our young people; a recent visiting team carried glowing reports of her work. Titus 2:3–5 calls the older women to train the younger women. This is an important part of our vision. Other mission workers such as Liz in Hong Kong and Linda in Amsterdam are young women who were also sent under the prayer, prophetic direction and covering of the elders. All three have sacrificed their careers to serve God.

Our church administrator, Gina, was responsible for many national conferences before going on to be the PA to Barney Coombs, Salt and Light Ministries, which is an international work.

'What about the men?' is the cry! Ten have given from three months up to a year of their time to serve the Lord in various places around the world. Tim and Rod both worked in China, teaching English in higher institutions and leading people to Christ in their spare time. Tim, who is 30 and fluent in Mandarin, was the first single person to lead an overseas team, which last year went into China. Several of that team now have a vision for longer-term work.

We vary long- and short-term mission in the church; many teams only go for a two- or three-week period. Anyone who can faithfully raise the finances and can contribute to the team's work is encouraged to pray about joining up. Last year we had teams in Europe, Africa and Asia. Age is no barrier—one of our oldest participants was a 73-year-old widower and my son at 2+ was one of the youngest! Delia, widowed several years ago and our church secretary, has proved a great preacher on our Zimbabwe teams. She is an inspiration to team members and to the schools and churches that we minister in. Delia runs her own Bible studies for working women. It has been wonderful to see God using her talents to build up the church.

Role of the Leaders

We encourage the church to be seeking God to discover which areas He would have them serve and function in locally, nationally and internationally in line with the overall Antioch call. When individuals feel they have some picture of God's requirements they come to the full-time leaders. These leaders meet daily as a presbytery for prayer. We listen to their direction and in an atmosphere of praise, prayer and worship seek God's direction along with them.

When God has clearly spoken, we get alongside them with their local congregations and send them out with prayer, support and covering into the areas God has directed. This is often done at an overall church monthly celebration with the laying on of hands by the elders and prophecy being expected as in 1 Timothy 1:18, 1 Timothy 4:14 and 2 Timothy 1:6–7. This is a very vital part of ministry because it gives recognition, accountability, validation and support. We review this when workers return for a break because communication is always in danger of developing 'gremlins' and finances and prayer covering always need updating.

Personal Growth

It is amazing to see the growth of people when they go into another culture on one of the teams. Over 100 people have been on teams to Zimbabwe in eight years (42 have been single). The last team was small, a dozen people, five of whom were single people. We covered over 75 meetings in a ten-day period in heat to which many were not accustomed. Often I was away from the team; one Sunday they managed fourteen meetings. So guess who was speaking? They were! To see their joy at being used by the Lord to lead people to Christ, to pray for the sick, to watch people getting filled with the Spirit, in school, SU groups and local churches was great. To be with them going 'door to door' in the mud hut village of Churu outside Harare, helping a pastor to plant a new church, was a thrill for me. To witness them sharing Jesus in the beer hall and praying for people gave me a glimpse of the joy that goes on in the Father's heart when He sees His children realising their potential in Him.

These team members have had to raise £800 by faith, get time off work, then face heat, challenging situations, languages and demands they have never known. On top of this they have preached probably more than they have ever done before and moved in the supernatural in ways they would never have believed possible. And God delights in using them! One girl began using words of knowledge accurately there and this is continuing at home. Another moved powerfully in evangelism and exhortation and is now being used by the Lord in her growing house church. Others found themselves speaking to hundreds, having previously spoken only in a house group.

What happens when they come home? Many who served on overseas teams as single people in the '70s and '80s are now in significant leadership roles here and elsewhere. Exposure brings growth. Yes, it's hair-raising at times but it also raises new ministries, so the risk is always worth it. So is the cost!

The King's School

With people constantly coming and going on the Antioch call and with our Christian school continually being exposed to brothers and sisters from abroad, it is little wonder so many end up going on mission. That was God's directive to us in 1981 as we began the school.

The King's School has at present 148 pupils and has been running for eleven years. It is a faith school, supported by sacrificial giving by the church members. We try to use the very best teachers who will be a model of godliness, not just education, for our children. There are six full-time staff, three of whom are single, six part-time and 50 more give their time freely.

The three single women in the school were all specially chosen by the elders as women who could not only teach but also train and disciple. Each is recognised in the church as having become a model whom others can follow. Like their elders they are not perfect, but they give a lead in faith, prayer, teaching and worship to our young people and they are held in love and respect by the church. They also have significant ministries across the church and each has travelled in ministry abroad. Their godly influence has already affected hundreds of children's and parents' lives. One, Dee, spent two years in full-time pastoral work in the church, on her return from Bible school, before moving into the school.

Again, the time, energy and talents these single people had were what set them apart, not their singleness.

Schools Evangelism

Our full-time schools evangelism team has had five single people in it under Gary's leadership. Gary (recently married) and his team have worked in Spain, Zimbabwe and The Gambia as well as the UK, and are currently working in over 40 of the 54 schools in our area. This team, Centrestage, all under 26 years of age, has been a real inspiration both to our own young people and other churches in the country.

Centrestage is responsible for school assemblies, CU meetings and lessons, and spends its time helping children to understand spiritual truths. It is a very creative team with excellent drama and musical skills, presenting their message to a generation which doesn't hear it. God has given them favour with schools and staff and it has been a valuable investment of our resources. It also shows our younger people that full-time workers are not always of pensionable age with short haircuts and suits. Gary's long, flowing ginger hair and outrageous shirts give the lie to that impression! The team has also given much needed encouragement to our Christian state school teachers, who often labour alone. Faith has also had to be exercised by this team for their finances, which has been a journey of excitement for them and for us.

Training and Discipleship

It is really vital that in our churches we are constantly encouraging and developing the gifts that lie hidden in our midst. Most people only ever fulfil 15 per cent of their potential. This is a tragedy. With this in mind we are constantly running training programmes. The prophets train the prophets, teachers share the teaching gifts, etc., and so you will find many young single people in all our training programmes, having their gifts developed by maturer ministries. Discipleship groups meet regularly over periods of a year at a time where maturer Christians train married and single people with a view to strengthening the saints and the congregations. Our goal is to have 'each part working properly' so the Body can grow up to be like Jesus!

One area from which we have seen excellent fruit is taking young people full-time into our team in our pastoral base at the National Westminster Bank we bought. These men were funded by their faith walk and by tithes. Alan worked for a year as a 'Timothy' in training, then went to Canada to Bible school and now heads up a youth work project. Richard was with us for two years, then went back to study agriculture. He is now a married man working full-time, sent out from us to run the orphanage and farm in Uganda. Tim was with us for a year and then had eighteen months full-time in China. At present we have a young 'trainee' evangelist Mark, who is only eighteen months old in the Lord. He is being trained daily amongst our full-time leaders and to keep his feet on the ground he works two days a week in the Christian school. The Centrestage schools team has been similarly funded from tithes, with two men and three girls on it, and they too have been a real blessing in modelling ministry. Working alongside the full-time leaders they grow in gifting and keep us in touch with younger areas of society.

People's age or status is irrelevant. What is important is: is God speaking to us through them, and is God using them?

Local Congregations

What about the local congregations? Well, here and in the house groups is where all of our ministry finds its training ground. A church like ours is not always comfortable to be in because we keep planting new congregations. There is little room to hide because everyone is needed to work. If you don't work in the school or the pastoral base, if you don't work with the youth, if you don't work in the Pregnancy Crisis Centre (which sees 1,000 women a year) then you're bound to get caught sooner or later in our congregational net!

Phil was 22 and single when he began to plant a new congregation. He and Helen married eighteen months later, by which time he was leading the new church. It now has over 50 members and Phil's maxim is 'If this church doesn't grow and work, then it's everyone's fault!' Phil insisted everyone took part and I'm amazed how they've shared the preaching, teaching, caring and worship. 'We've had to!' is their honest reply. This group has probably the highest proportion of single people in ministry. Two help lead the Startrite group for new believers (there are many!), one leads the evangelism and the administrator is also single. They also already have three couples in mission overseas and this church is only four years old!

Phil has sat with the elders from the start and contributes with the best of them. He and many others give us great joy because they are sons and daughters born in our house. They have been trained on our Timothy Camps for young men, on Chosen Women weeks and through our discipleship groups. When you see the products of your training now training others who are faithful (2 Tim. 2:1–2), then you rejoice.

Our progress can only be measured in our successors. There is always a need for more—there are always weaknesses, but God gives the growth. I find many people want a big place or a big ministry without first having proved faithful in little things. Single people—all people for that matter—are encouraged to pray, to read the Bible, to move out in faith in spiritual gifts, to serve, to care and to witness. Out of this we then begin, as maturer leaders, to spot the gifts and graces and *then to make room for them*. Leaders need to be door openers, not door closers, making room for others to minister. Does this happen in your church? It needs to if the Body of Christ is to grow.

Widows, single parents, divorcees and older folk also have a role to play and you find them popping up in all areas: the Christian school, the Pregnancy Crisis Centre and the Jubilees work (over-65s). The Jubilees are a major joy; they are our prayer warriors, led by Pat, a widow, and one of our deacons. They are a source of encouragement to us all. Much of my own prayer support as I travel comes from them. Their wisdom and presence benefit the school and the leaders. One of our single parents has a vision from the Lord to be a 'mother with the Father's heart to the fatherless', and has been working it out practically. Some are prayer partners to the Pregnancy Crisis Centre counsellors and some are just grannies and grandads to us!

Listening to Each Other

Last year we decided to gather all our single folk together for a twelve-week series on issues affecting singles. My wife, Chris, and I met for several sessions over six months with a group of a dozen single people of all ages and worked out our strategy. I was to chair the meetings; they were to speak on issues that were vital to them. They brought back their messages and we worked on them together, then began the series.

Between 70 and 100 attended the series. Each week we had a few testimonies to encourage each other, a message, a coffee break, then discussion groups reporting back at the end. The ministry was excellent. The discussions were not always easy because of age range, and such a varied group of experiences and needs (16 to 75 years). Soon each particular grouping began to appreciate each other. The older people appreciated the young people's zeal for God; the youngsters appreciated the pain faced by deserted husbands or wives. The issues of loneliness and not fitting in were also faced. The discussion group leaders, different every week, discovered just how tough it can be to lead a group. It stretched us as a people.

I thoroughly enjoyed it, realising more and more the gold God had given us in our people. It was a thrilling experience for me. It didn't answer all our questions, it didn't give us all the answers, but it was a start. Although as I wrote this I thought it was almost too good to be true, it is not all raging success! We do have folk who have still not found their place, who are still frustrated in knowing what they should do, and folk who still struggle with their identity, but we are making progress, and our hope is that together we can work for the Kingdom and help each other be useful to the Lord in all His purposes.

And where did we take what we had learned in these teaching sessions, you might ask? Back to the local church where it all belongs. There were no special 'Singles Sundays'! No 'statutory single on everything' but a renewed hope that we would each discover our place and minister faithfully in it. And has it worked? To a degree—yes. As I look around now I see people growing in confidence in God's calling upon them. Regularly I hear of single folk having been used by the Lord in their local church, on the streets, in the evangelism team prowling the local ten-pin bowling-alley and ice-rink.

A Last Look Around

I was visiting the Chineham congregation as they sent out eighteen-year-old Karen to work with street children in Calcutta. She was to be based in an orphanage for a year. Her mother Beryl has herself served the Lord in India, and Karen is another product of our Christian school! It was a joy to hear her father bringing God's Word over her and the church standing to send her out.

I looked around the congregation and noticed one of the worship leaders was a young single man, as was the administrator. We went on to have lunch at our secretary Delia's house. She is, as I've said earlier, a widow and a Zimbabwe team veteran. Three of the issues we discussed were: writing this chapter; whether she would help lead on the Zimbabwe team this year by discipling some of the younger members; and the next gathering of 'Harvest', a monthly group for women across our town to be encouraged to grow in the Lord. Delia and Beryl, another single lady in the church, with my wife and others, are a part of that team. Then I thought of Beryl. It was she who produced our 'First Steps Bible Studies' for our new believers and I suddenly realised there is no end to single people being used where you find a willing heart to be a servant of God.

What then am I, as the senior pastor, looking for across the church? Well, you don't have to be married or single to minister, but you have to be obedient, willing, ready and faithful—it also helps if you are anointed! Availability and action are the order of the day. God longs for models that His people can imitate. He wants 'doers not dreamers', 'workers not wanderers', 'warriors not worriers' and He wants pastors to be constantly calling up their labourers to 'hear and do, not just to listen and watch'!

---

[1] From Cassidy, M., *Bursting the Wineskins* (London: Hodder & Stoughton, 1983).

10

Facing the Future

Unless the Christian desires above all else to be totally possessed by charity, unless he allows himself to be enflamed with the love of Jesus Christ, he will not be able to persist in either true marriage or true celibacy.

Roger Schutz, Prior of Taizé
in Foreword to *Marriage and Celibacy*

If the statisticians are to be believed, by the year 2021, a staggering 45 per cent of British adults will be single. Barring a great and unexpected reversal, the number of single people in our society and, therefore, in our churches is to continue rising.

On a range of issues, the church has too often found itself reacting to change after it has happened, rather than in anticipation. With a major long-term demographic shift in progress, we have time to make the changes necessary, but we must begin to act now.

An Eight-stage Strategy for the Local Church

Stage One: Significance
We start by acknowledging, both personally and as churches, that singleness is an important issue and

affirming the significance of every single member of our congregations regardless of marital status. As part of Sunday worship a local church could arrange a public act of commitment, in which those who are married and those who are single repent of wrong attitudes to each other and commit themselves to love and support each other in prayer and service. This may help breed the vision for a new way of being the church together, families and singles of all kinds, side by side, equally at home in the Kingdom of God.

Stage Two: Survey
Until they sit down and think about it, most church leaders do not know how many single people are members of their own church. Research the facts, conduct a survey of church members to discover their perspective on singleness. Do the married couples regard themselves as somehow superior? What do the single people think of the sermon illustrations? Would they like something especially for them? How do the different types of single people view the church? Which reactions do they have in common? Which are divergent?

In most churches taking action requires that a large number of people are convinced that change is necessary. The results of an initial survey can provide crucial evidence to help those who are married to see issues from the singles' perspective. Use the recommendations in Appendix A as a checklist for self-evaluation.

Stage Three: Scripture
Much space has been given in this book to an investigation of singleness in Scripture. Many

congregations have never heard the subject preached or taught. If a corrective to our thinking is necessary, then it is the Bible that must be our guide. The *Singularly Significant* Bible study series could be used as house group material for all the church, in conjunction with Sunday sermons, to create a platform for action. Also the 'Sixteen Myths about Celibacy and Marriage' listed in Appendix B can be a useful basis for married and single people to discuss together and better understand each other's situation.

It is not just teaching on singleness which is necessary. It is equally important that as Scripture is regularly taught in the church, the applications given are relevant to singles as well as families. This is not to suggest that family illustrations are invalid, but they need to be balanced by others that apply to those who live alone, or reworked to apply to the wider cross-sections of life styles represented in the congregation.

There is one specific issue which must be faced, however difficult it may be. Every church should know where it stands on the issue of divorce and remarriage. The number of divorcees in our ranks is certain to continue growing. Evangelical Christians disagree over the interpretation of Scripture, but each congregation needs to agree a policy which can be consistently implemented. Different churches are likely to come to different conclusions. Clarity will prevent those who are single again following a divorce getting confused and hurt even more.

Stage Four: Structures
Single people often complain that their voice is not heard. If a church has an exclusively married

leadership, this can easily be the case. Neither marriage nor celibacy are in themselves qualifications for leadership. This is not an issue of democracy: it is a plea to recognise the gifts and calling of all, regardless of marital status. If a church has an all-married church council or eldership because there is no suitable single person, this need not be a problem, just as long as the church would be equally content with an all-single leadership! It is the unspoken assumption that leaders must be married that is wrong.

There is a deeply embedded assumption afflicting both church and much of society, that true maturity comes through marriage and parenthood, and that until someone has successfully negotiated these two hurdles they are not really fit for responsibility and leadership. Marriage and parenthood are both demanding and can hasten maturity. In 1 Timothy 3:2–5 and 11–13 Paul makes it clear that both of these issues are crucial tests of a person's suitability for leadership. He does not say that these are the only tests. Maturity can be reached without marriage.

Many single people themselves need to understand this, as often they have made the same assumptions, even when they have highly responsible jobs. Spiritual maturity primarily comes through spending time alone with God and in serving His people. Emotional maturity for single people often comes once they have accepted themselves and their singleness, but this is such a highly personal issue that generalisation is difficult. The church can play a crucial role in helping its younger single people reach a degree of maturity, so that they can be fit to lead. This should be one of the goals of discipleship in a church.

Additionally, special interest groups such as

retired singles, divorcees, single parents and those recently bereaved, may appreciate the opportunity to meet together regularly. The numbers may be small and the integration of these groups into existing structures of the church relatively easy. The hardest part is often taking the initiative. The fruit can be impressive.

In the event of an all-married group 'at the top', (or, to be more faithful to a biblical view of leadership, supporting 'from the bottom'), some open channel of communication should be established so that the legitimate concerns of the singles in the church can be heard. It is the unintentional discrimination that hurts most single adults, not least in the choice of house group leaders. If a single man or woman is gifted to lead a group, they should not be barred because they do not have a suitable home to meet in. Another couple or single in this group can be the host/hostess.

Stage Five: Social Activities

In many churches, single people and married couples will have a very similar appreciation of the *spiritual* life of the church. Their views are more likely to be divergent concerning its *social* life. Families often find their social needs met through the regular activities, singles seldom do. Their needs are different. A singles group, or occasional programme of special events— barbecues, theatre trips, sporting activities, parties or the like—can provide a low-key, non-threatening way for single people to meet their peers, without stimulating unhelpful gossip. Social activities for singles form a necessary supplement to the church's wider social life.

There is a tension between the expressed desire of

the majority of single people not to be labelled 'the singles', and meeting their legitimate social needs. They dislike the title 'single' because, sadly, there is a stigma attached to it. Singles groups are perceived to consist entirely of those desperate for a partner. Christian singleness requires a new, positive image.

Single people of both sexes enjoy developing friendships with families. They often enjoy the company of children. This desire for social integration need not be compromised if a church also arranges for single people to meet with their peers for social activity. Christian single people need the right environment to meet each other, to share common needs and to strengthen each other. If in the process they meet a prospective partner and a relationship develops naturally as a result, praise God for that.

The church also needs actively to encourage both families and single people to include each other into their own social lives. This can include invites to Sunday lunch, leisure trips, parties, holidays, etc. Married couples *must* resist most strongly the temptation to matchmake. Well-meaning Christian couples have caused so much heartache, frustration and embarrassment in the past through inviting two eligible people to dinner in the hope that romance will blossom. There is safety in numbers, all numbers that is, except one plus one!

Stage Six: Sexuality

If we ignore the sexual side of a single person we deny part of their humanity, part of what God created them to be. Merely to repeat the commands of Scripture is not enough. Many single churchgoers struggle with temptation. They know what is right and wrong, but feel weak. There is great sexual pressure on the single person in a society which demonstrates almost no restraint. We must be enablers as well as prophets. We should continue to speak out on the moral issues of our age, but in parallel with practical help for its victims.

The gap between sexual behaviour of secular young people and their Christian counterparts is narrowing, and not because non-Christians are becoming biblical! Christians are under such pressure that moral compromise is common—first in practice, then in principle. In a recent survey of secular youth clubs by Frontier Youth Trust and Brunel University they found that less than one in ten of those under 21 thought it important to remain a virgin until marriage, compared to eight out of ten church members. Many Christian young single people are no longer virgins, even if they believe they should be. They were not able to resist the temptation when it came. The second time it is even more difficult to say 'no'. After a while of failing to live according to what we believe, it is easier to change our beliefs than our behaviour. Increasingly, some singles are denying the need for celibacy. This accords with their actions: it does not accord with Scripture.

If a person is converted after being sexually active they may have to work hard at their celibacy. Whether it is a virgin who wonders what the grass is like on the other side, or someone who is sexually experienced and has times of longing for past intimacy, they need help.

A place and a time where single Christians can be open and honest with one another about their sexual struggles is essential. They must not be left to soldier alone. Those who battle with homosexuality and lesbianism may find it especially difficult to talk about their feelings, yet may be those who would benefit most by doing so.

Both in principle and in practice, single adults need help to work out their sexuality in accordance with Scripture and in contravention of the expectations of society. The church must not fail its single members.

Stage Seven: Society

If we have so many lonely single people in the church, what hope do we have to offer the non-Christian single? Our goal in putting things right in our own back yard is not that it may be clean and tidy, but that it is ready to be invaded from outside. As yet, we have made little progress in reaching many of the single people in the world with the gospel. Single people are a difficult group to target. We must make the church inviting to them, and preach a gospel which is relevant to their needs. Our singles reformation is not just to sort ourselves out, but must be to prepare the ground for a great awakening amongst the singles in society. The church, above all, is the one place they *should* be attracted to. It offers them belonging, comfort, healthy relationships, love and security as free gifts, all accompanying the main item of salvation. We preach Christ, the perfect single man, who drew all men to Him (John 12:32). As He gathered the lonely and outcast of His day, so through us, their twentieth-century singles equivalent can find Him too.

Stage Eight: Service

Throughout history single people have a wonderful record of Christian service. As we have seen in the early church, many leaders were voluntarily single in order to serve God better. Calvin and the reformers encouraged singleness as long as it was a personal decision, not one of compulsion as in the Roman Catholic church. The missionary movements of the nineteenth and twentieth centuries relied to a considerable extent on single people, especially women.

The future should be no different. A fresh vision for Christian single people serving the Lord in all different capacities is needed. The options are vast. Within the local congregation there are many responsible positions that single people may well be able to fulfil better than married people, particularly if they can be freed from more mundane responsibilities. Single people may not have any more time than their married counterparts, but they do generally have more flexibility.

Short-term missionary service has become a favourite outlet for many young single people. Organisations such as Operation Mobilisation with their Love Europe summer programme of evangelism and year-long teams, Youth With A Mission, Oasis, International Teams and many others offer wonderful opportunities for young people to learn, through working in a different environment, new skills and abilities which can be invaluable to any church. More churches should actively encourage their singles to go on these programmes and financially support them to do it.

Older single people can get involved too. Many missions and Christian organisations are constantly looking for mature people to fill key roles. Some can take early retirement or extended leave of absence from their jobs to serve in this way. In all cases the role of the local church is of crucial importance; it should not be left solely to the individual to take the initiative. 'God bless you, brother' and a pat on the shoulder is not enough!

Our horizon must not stop there. There is a real need for long-term workers who are single. Those who choose to be single for the sake of the Kingdom of God are worthy of the greatest respect rather than sympathy. They may find themselves in the most inhospitable of places, where it would be unwise for a family with young children to be. They may work long hours doing demanding jobs behind the scenes. In the missionary teams in the New Testament there were many single workers. Most single Christian workers today, whether in a local church or a missionary situation, prefer to be part of a team. All the advantages that Paul outlined of single people serving God still apply. The application may be different; the principle is not.

As a strategic resource, as opposed to a convenient one, the British church is guilty of failing to utilise its single people properly in the service of God. This must be reconsidered urgently.

There are three important areas where change is needed that lie outside the direct responsibility of the local church.

1. Extended families
Appropriate housing is an issue for many single people. A great many singles enjoy living on their own, but a large number find this too lonely an existence.

Single people sharing a house/flat together is one option, but is often an unstable arrangement. Some UK building societies have become reluctant to loan mortgages to such households because of the lack of security. Long-term singles with no intention to marry and who are close friends may make a 'David and

Jonathan' style commitment to each other which involves shared accommodation.

Communities of committed single celibates formed for the purpose of prayer and service (often, also with a shared commitment to a simple life style) can provide a short-term place of refuge and recovery for singles damaged by past experiences, as well as good support and relationships for its long-term core members. Initial experiments in the USA and UK need to be reproduced and lessons learned from their experiences.

The most common arrangement is that of an extended family. Many couples and families have an empty room which could provide a secure home for a single person. Particularly younger singles, for whom it is no longer appropriate or possible to live in their parental home, would still prefer to live in a family environment. Many well-adjusted singles, as well as some who are hurt and damaged, like the combination of freedom and security, independence and limited responsibility that this provides. It should be an enriching experience for the hosts as well as the guests. Clive and Ruth Calver have opened their home to a variety of single people through the years. Ruth writes:

> The whole concept of 'open homes' should be an essential part of our Christian lives. The early church was especially noted for its community life. All the believers were together and had everything in common . . . They broke bread in their homes and ate together with glad and sincere hearts (Acts 2:44–46). In Romans 12:13 we are all instructed to 'Share with God's people who are in need. Practise hospitality.'

A commitment to hospitality stems from hearts which are open to God and desire homes open to service. This can easily become a contagious habit, especially when it is first practised by those in positions of leadership in the church.

Sometimes the Lord requires us to go further than just having our homes open for meals. He asks us to invite others to live with us. [For us] at first they tended to be young people in Christian work, and then in more recent years those who were struggling to work out their Christian lives against a background perhaps of sexual abuse, family break-up or some other disadvantage.

There can be a lot of extra work, and some heartache, but also a great deal of fun. From personal experience there can be such joy in incorporating others into our homes. The lives of our children can be deepened, perhaps to realise how well off they are as far as family stability and spiritual input are concerned. When we allow them to share in the suffering and difficulties other people experience, then they can develop a natural empathy for the needs of others.[1]

2. Inter-church singles groups

In Britain there is a reluctance amongst many single Christians to consider singles groups. They have a bad image. In the USA singles groups are regarded much more positively. An all-age Sunday school programme will probably include a class for single adults. There may be a first-class social programme attached which is envied by their married peers. Large churches have singles pastors—specifically responsible for all single adults in the church.

European culture is different. The local church is generally smaller. If a Christian single man wants to meet a Christian single woman but comes from a small church he has a problem. His own church does not have enough people to sustain a group. However, if a programme of events exists, worthwhile in its own right and arranged on an inter-church basis with good leadership, this can be of great benefit to many lonely adults. It should not be *primarily* about finding a partner, even if that is the motivation of some attending—it should be about meeting the need for friendship amongst peers, and enjoying the good things of life. It need make no demands to hinder commitment to the local church, but can positively relieve a pressure point.

The concept needs to be given a chance to work. Too much 'it'll never work here' mentality can hinder us learning from a model that is working successfully in America.

3. Pastoral training

Recently I was invited to give a guest lecture on singleness at a well-known theological college in the UK as part of their pastoral studies course. It was the first time that the subject had ever been included in the syllabus. Most ministerial students are totally untrained for pastoring the single people in their future congregations.

Ministerial training must in future give due consideration to the issue of singleness. A theology of singleness should be taught alongside the theology of marriage. Practical and theoretical material should be included in the pastoral theology course, whether in a post-graduate year as favoured by some colleges or in an integrated manner as currently practised by most.

As the overwhelming majority of those accepted for ministerial training are married men, there is a great likelihood that they will be totally unprepared for the real problems of single people. They are less likely to recognise the potential of the singles within their church and unready to correct unconscious prejudice within their congregations. It is inconceivable that any other group with the church amounting to one-third of all adults could be so ignored by our present training.

A Dream

I have a dream of a nation in which all churches esteem single adults as equal to those who are married. A dream of single people taking their role in leadership at all levels. A dream of great relationships between married and single people, old and young. One where burdens are shared, homes are open and needs are met. A dream where divorcees, single parents, widows and widowers all receive lots of love and support. A dream where single people meet together without gossip of relationships and pressure to pair up. A dream where single people are living holy lives, supporting one another to shine as lights in the darkness and avoiding all moral compromise. A dream where Christians of all kinds understand the strategic role that single people can have in Christian service at home and overseas. A dream where those committed to a celibate life are respected, not pitied.

Last Word

In the first chapter, a cross-section of single people from one local church shared their own experience of singleness. Additionally they were asked, 'What one thing would you like to say to church leaders about being single?' These are some of their replies. It is appropriate to leave the last word to them.

- 'Remember Jesus was single.'
- 'We are as important as couples.'
- 'Help me to realise my potential in the service of God.'
- 'I find it hard being single.'
- 'The church must always consider all groups—married people, children, who are often mentioned, and single people.'
- 'It is a valid calling.'
- 'The person who is single for a long time will have weaknesses and problems unique to their station, and I would ask church leaders to be sensitive and supportive.'
- 'As a single person one has to work hard at becoming integrated into the church family.'
- 'Marriage is not necessarily a superior status.'

---

[1]*Renewal* No. 189, February 1992.